INTRODUCTION TO KINSHIP AND SOCIAL ORGANIZATION

Burton Pasternak

Hunter College, City University of New York

PRENTICE-HALL, INC., Englewood Cliffs, New Jersey

Library of Congress Cataloging in Publication Data

PASTERNAK, BURTON.
  Introduction to kinship and social organization.

  (Prentice-Hall series in anthropology)
  Bibliography: p.
  Includes index.
  1. Social structure. 2. Kinship. I. Title.
GN490.P38   301.42'1   75-20135
ISBN   0-13-485474-8
ISBN   0-13-485466-7 pbk.

Prentice-Hall Series in Anthropology

DAVID M. SCHNEIDER, Editor

Printed in the United States of America

10 9 8 7 6 5 4 3 2 1

Prentice-Hall International, Inc., *London*
Prentice-Hall of Australia, Pty. Ltd., *Sydney*
Prentice-Hall of Canada, Ltd., *Toronto*
Prentice-Hall of India Private Limited, *New Delhi*
Prentice-Hall of Japan, Inc., *Tokyo*
Prentice-Hall of Southeast Asia (Pte.) Ltd., *Singapore*

To
Alex, Bryn,
and
Red-The-Mad

Contents

3

INCEST REGULATIONS 28

4

RULES OF POSTMARITAL RESIDENCE 42

5

FORMS OF MARRIAGE 58

6

REGULATION ON MARRIAGE 66

7

THE FAMILY 82

8

THE PRINCIPLES AND STRUCTURES OF DESCENT   101

9

SYSTEMS OF KINSHIP NOMENCLATURE   124

Acknowledgments

Since I am willing to accept, without reservation, whatever credit may accrue from this modest effort, I am obliged to also assume responsibility for whatever flaws, errors, or oversights it may contain. While the defects are entirely my own doing, I cannot claim sole credit for whatever may be of value and interest in this book. Apart from the myriad of scholars whose intellectual contributions I have attempted to summarize, I also owe a debt to those who took a personal and direct hand in igniting whatever intellectual fires burn within me—in particular, to my teachers John Landgraf, Merton H. Fried, and Marvin Harris, and to the many scholars from whom I subsequently profited through interaction and discussion. A social expression of gratitude is due my colleagues Carol R. Ember, Melvin Ember, and Daniel Gross for their painstaking and generous readings of early versions of this manuscript and for their constructive suggestions, criticisms, and constant encouragement. Thanks are due Marguerite Fabio for having labored with the typing of various versions of this manuscript, and to the editorial staff of Prentice-Hall, and to Edward H. Stanford in particular, for the guidance and help they provided.

It is appropriate that I conclude with a singular expression of gratitude to my companion, Brigitte, without whose insight and patience this book might have remained forever on the back-burner. It was her special knack for asking hard, honest questions in the gentlest possible way that really brought this book to life.

1

Introduction

This book is concerned with the kinds of social relationships entered into by individuals and groups, past and present. It is an introduction to basic concepts and problems of human social organization. Human behavior is viewed as not random, accidental, or whimsical but rather as the patterned and predictable result of knowable causes. It is assumed that even when people are not aware of what they do or why, their social behavior is to a large extent shaped by, and responsive to, the physical and technological conditions under which they live. The perspective employed in this book is evolutionary—human society has become increasingly complex over time and the nature and the sources of this development are of interest to us. We recognize that there may be innate limits to the ways in which humans can and do organize themselves—thresholds beyond which people cannot go. But within these limits humankind has demonstrated enormous flexibility and innovative talent. In short, our focus in the chapters that follow will be upon the nature, extent, and probable causes of social variation.

On the Primate Origins of Human Sociality

In recent years a number of authors have suggested that we view human social behavior against the backdrop of our primate origins and heritage.

1

They have stressed the "animal nature" of humankind (cf., Ardrey 1961, 1966, 1970; Lorenz 1966; Morris 1967); some even claiming that, like other primates with whom we share a common origin, we are fundamentally and naturally territorial, aggressive animals. Some propose that one of the basic functions of human culture, indeed, is to channel and deflect such primate propensities in a constructive and adaptive direction. Because such claims have become fashionable in recent years, it would be useful to precede our inquiry into the nature and varieties of human social organization with some consideration of the social behavior of subhuman primates and of the relevance of that behavior for an understanding of human social behavior.

Most primates form social groups the members of which relate to each other in a systematic, structured way.[1] It is now quite certain that much primate social behavior is not imprinted or physiologically determined; all primates learn and all acquire familiarity with social roles and expectations in the course of interacting. The importance of learning has been determined both experimentally and in the observation of free-ranging animals. Experiment has taught us, for example, that when immature monkeys are prevented from interaction or if they are isolated with their mothers and cannot observe adult interactions, they usually turn out to be social misfits as adults. While normal monkeys have a genetic capacity for proper adult social behavior, the realization of that capacity requires learning. Differences in learning similarly account for the fact that some groups of macaque monkeys, in the wild, developed the habit of washing sweet potatoes before eating them, and learned to separate wheat from sand by dropping the two in water so that the heavier sand could drop out (Itani 1961; Kummer 1971: 117–124; and Southwick 1972).

Although the social behavior of all primates depends, to some extent, upon learning and experience subhuman primate learning tends to be mainly situation-bound. Only humans commonly and easily learn at a distance—an ability that is undoubtedly related to the special circuitry and capacities of the human brain. If I report, for example, that I fell ill upon eating a can of Brand X chow mein I may persuade you to avoid Brand X; it is not essential that you personally witness the sequence of events. Our capacity for such learning is facilitated by a communication system that, in contrast to those employed by other primates, is highly referential. Language makes it possible for us to refer to things not involved in our immediate interaction situation or within our vision. We can discuss events of the past, events that might occur at some future time, or events that

---

[1] For an excellent review and summary of the literature on primate social behavior and its underpinnings see Kummer 1971 and Southwick 1972. For anthropological rebuttals to those who stress the aggressive, territorial, and primate nature of humankind see the aforementioned works, Alland 1972, or Montagu 1968.

could not possibly take place. If I invite you to imagine a yellow polka-dot cloud you can do so although you would not expect to ever see one.

Granting that primate social behavior is at least in part learned, let us consider more closely the nature of that behavior. What are the general characteristics of nonhuman social organization? For one thing, animals usually arrange themselves in some sort of hierarchy. Certain males enjoy prior access to food and sometimes (although not invariably) to females in heat. Some writers have unduly stressed the importance of dominance hierarchies in nonhuman primate groups and have exaggerated the role of aggression and physical force in establishing relative position within such hierarchies. One reason for the impression that primates are naturally very aggressive has been that, until recently, most of our observations had been made of animals confined to zoo cages which, like human prisons, significantly alter and color the behavior of their inhabitants. Recent studies of primates in the wild indicate that leadership does not depend entirely upon brute force. While the leader of a primate group is often the strongest male, this is not always the case; sometimes it is the oldest male that exerts principal authority and leadership. Studies of free-ranging primates also indicate that group leaders actually devote very little time to assaulting other animals; once a dominance hierarchy has been established, aggression is most commonly avoided or short-circuited. It should also be noted that among some species it is difficult to detect a clearly defined dominance hierarchy.

Those among us who, confronted by daily reminders of humankind's capacity for "inhuman" behavior, have found some comfort in the belief that, after all, men will be primates, will no doubt be disturbed by the discovery that nonhuman primates are usually quite affable and peaceful creatures. The erroneous and unjust impression that many of us harbor about our closest primate relatives, the gorilla and the chimpanzee, has been as much influenced by Hollywood propaganda as by the observation of captive animals, so it is not surprising that whenever the word "gorilla" is uttered many of us reflexively envision fierce, big-toothed beasts carrying negligee-clad damsels off into dank swamps. Fictional and even some supposedly nonfictional portrayals often cast the nonhuman primates in the roles of hunters and killers. It is time that the reputations of our long-maligned and less articulate relatives be repaired and restored. The truth, unexciting though it may be, is that most of the nonhuman primates are generally unaggressive. If the *human* primate is innately violent and aggressive (which is far from certain or established), then he is evidently distinctive among primates in this regard. Not only are the nonhuman primates rather gentle creatures, but they have an overwhelming dietary predilection for vegetables. Few species hunt animals, and those that do spend little time doing so and remain predominantly faithful to a vegetarian regime. Since most nonhuman primates confine their hunting and killing to plant life, the hunting and killing of animals by some humans is evidently not a manifestation of some general primate necessity or propensity.

It is true that nearly all primates are territorial in the sense that they tend to remain within certain areas most of the time. We once believed that nonhuman primates tolerated little or no territorial intrusion—that they were by nature territorially exclusive—and that a similar primate inclination underlies much of human behavior. However, it has recently been discovered that many nonhuman primates operate in terms of rather flexible territorial boundaries and tend to be tolerant of trespass. If humans are territorially exclusive by instinct or nature, then, they may be unusual among primates in this regard as well.

Probably the most striking and most important discovery that has emerged from the study of free-ranging primates is that they manifest great behavioral variation *within* as well as between species. The frequency of aggressive displays or threats, the degree to which animals exhibit territoriality, and even the form, size, and structure of groups have all been found to vary in terms of environmental conditions. Current knowledge of the nonhuman primates suggests that multianimal groups and general sociability have definite adaptive value. Grouping is useful for reproductive success, for defense against predators, for warning against dangers, for locating sources of food, etc. It also appears that groups of different size, composition, and organization are selected for in different environments. To say that animals are capable of responding to changes in their environment by adjusting their behavior is not to deny a genetic input or a physiological constraint upon behavior. Animals certainly adjust to environmental demands in terms of genetic givens—gorillas can't escape predators by growing wings and taking flight. Genetic givens may change over the long haul but in response to immediate exigencies the primates (and especially humans) are also capable of nongenetic adaptations—behavioral adjustments that can be learned and transmitted extrasomatically.

We are still sorting the biological givens from behavioral traditions that primates acquire through learning, but one thing is already quite clear: of all the primates humankind enjoys the greatest capacity for extrasomatic adjustment to changing circumstances and new requirements. While we have not grown wings we have nevertheless acquired an ability to fly. We have done so not by defying our physical limitations but by observing and learning from animals whose biological givens provide the capacity for flight.

Since all humans are constrained by much the same genetic limitations it is unlikely that focusing on these constants will carry us very far in explaining and accounting for cultural variation. That primates (human and nonhuman) sometimes act aggressively, that they may be territorially exclusive, hunt or kill each other proves only that they have a capacity for such behavior—that their bodies and genetic inventories provide the necessary circuitry and equipment. But primates also have the circuitry for peacefulness, territorial flexibility, cooperation, and self-sacrifice. Which biological capacity or option will be realized depends, to a large extent, on the conditions under which animals find themselves. As social scientists we must take the biological capacities of humankind as givens and then ferret out the conditions that are likely to predispose a particular people or group of people to activate one possible response or another.

"Explaining" the Social Nature of Humankind

If the primate nature of people cannot satisfactorily account for similarities and differences in the way they organize themselves, how then shall we go about explaining these variations? As a starting point we can explore the relationship among the rules that men generate to define "appropriate" behavior, observations as to what people believe they do, and what they actually do in many ethnographically described societies. We can then formulate logically consistent hypotheses as to which phenomena (rules, beliefs, or occurrences) are related and in what ways. When making intersocietal comparisons it is vital that we keep in mind that the ideas people have about what constitutes "proper" behavior may differ from their beliefs about what people normally do. And since both ideal and presumed behavior may differ from real or actual behavior, we must be sure that comparisons are in terms of a common behavioral aspect (see Richards 1969 and Josselin DeJong 1971). Merely proposing a "reasonable" explanation for some human behavior, however, does not fulfill our scientific obligation because not all good ideas are correct. Many a good idea about how one might construct a flying machine never got off the ground. The correctness of any interpretation should ultimately be put to an empirical test. If at all possible, explanations and hypotheses should be phrased in such a way that they can be projected against a sample of societies to see if the associations suggested actually occur with a frequency that would not be likely by chance or accident. Such statistical associations, once established and weighed against each other, lend support to suggested hypotheses and also enable us to reject ideas which have no predictive value.[2]

While all good ideas should be submitted to empirical validation if

[2] For a brief and simple description of how hypotheses may be framed and tested cross-culturally see Otterbein 1969. For a review and evaluation of the cross-cultural method, its potentialities, limitations, and accomplishments see Naroll 1970.

possible, not all logically consistent and persuasive explanations are amenable to such testing. A good idea or an interesting avenue of inquiry should not be abandoned simply because hope of empirical validation is foreclosed. There is no shame in speculation so long as we clearly distinguish ideas that are speculative from those that have achieved some measure of empirical support. In the chapters to follow we will confront a variety of problems and we will consider some of the major solutions that have been proposed for them. Wherever a reasonable idea or proposal also enjoys some empirical support we will make that clear.

We begin our inquiry into the forms and determinants of human social organization with a brief review of the general stages through which humankind has moved, and with some speculation as to the kinds of factors that might have contributed to different rates and routes of societal tranformation. Having highlighted aspects of social organization that reflect developing complexity in human society we will turn, in chapters 3 through 9, to a more detailed consideration of particular aspects of social organization. In these chapters we will focus upon differences in form and behavior and consider major attempts to account for such variation.

2

The Evolution of Human Society: Bands, Tribes, Chiefdoms, and States

Central to this chapter is the notion of "evolution"—the idea that culture in general and societies in particular change in a directional fashion. Refining a formulation proposed by Herbert Spencer, Robert Carneiro has defined "evolution" as,

> a change from a relatively indefinite, incoherent homogeneity to a relatively definite, coherent heterogeneity, through successive differentiations and integrations (1974: 90; cf., Spencer 1862: 216).

Implicit in this definition is the notion that development is neither fortuitous nor accidental, that there is something regular about it.

The biological model of evolution assumes that if we expose different groups of a single breeding population to diverse environments, these environments will select biological attributes befitting themselves and will weed out genetic qualities and traits that are maladaptive. As a result of this process of "natural selection," groups of the same species in different environments eventually begin to differ in terms of genetic characteristics and gene frequencies and, if there comes a point at which the animals that comprise different groups can no longer interbreed to produce fertile offspring, then the selection process has produced separate species. An important attribute of the biological model of evolution is that it stresses progressive differentiation and diversification through natural selection. Distinct species are genetically isolated; traits can no longer be exchanged or shared since populations comprising different species cannot interbreed to produce fertile offspring. It would simply not be possible for humans to acquire an ability to breathe under water by tapping the genetic inventory of fish. Nor is there any way for us to acquire from cows a genetic capacity to digest grass or from sheep the ability to grow wool directly on our skins, convenient and economical though these capabilities might be.

The biological model of evolution is different in crucial ways from models of cultural evolution employed by social scientists. These have in common the assumption that cultures, unlike biological species, *can* borrow and exchange traits—they can become similar or different in response to selective pressures. Anthropologists employ (at least) two complementary models to describe different aspects of the evolution of culture (see Sahlins 1960; cf., Carneiro 1974). The "general" model has to do with the sequence in which cultural forms have appeared in human history. The focus is on the evolution of *culture* rather than on the developmental trajectories of specific societies or groups of societies. It is assumed that, in the course of human development, society became progressively more specialized and complex, and that complex forms presume the prior appearance of simpler ones.[1] State-integrated societies presuppose the earlier existence, somewhere in the world, of chiefdoms which were presumably built upon still simpler tribes. Tribal integration could not have emerged had still simpler band-organized societies not preceded them. While humankind thus progressed from simple hunting-gathering bands to the state, not *all* peoples made it all the way; not all achieved the most complex form of societal integration (i.e., the state) and those that did, did not necessarily do so in precisely the same way. Some people disappeared along the way, some stagnated, others skipped stages, and still others slipped backward. But humankind made it. Societal integration became increasingly complex even if not necessarily in the same location, among the same people, or at the same speed (see Service 1960b).

Depending on the conditions under which they live, people "progress" or move from stage to stage in different ways and at different rates. There are many kinds of domestication, for example, and, as we shall see, the particular form a people employs may influence the kind of society they will live in. If we are especially interested in the developmental routes that particular societies or groups of societies have taken, or if we are interested in why some societies developed complex forms of societal integration while others didn't, or in why some people made the transition one way rather than another, then we must adopt a "specific" evolutionary

[1] For an excellent survey of cross-cultural studies which support the simple to complex evolutionary sequence see Naroll 1956.

perspective. In short, the "general" evolutionary model describes the stages through which CULTURE has passed while the "specific" model is concerned with the nature and sources of individual transformation.

In this chapter our task will be to trace the general societal stages through which humankind as a whole has moved, and to indicate some of the things that might have had an impact on the nature and rate of societal transformation. Our discussion is intended to establish a general framework within which we can examine particular aspects of kinship and social organization. In describing the evolution of human society from bands through tribes and chiefdoms to the state, we employ a conceptual framework established by Elman Service (1962). This sequential scheme is not the only one or even necessarily the best one; there are many ways in which the sweep of human societal development could usefully be perceived and described. But the particular features by means of which stages are distinguished here will serve our purpose, which is to indicate how human society has become larger, more heterogeneous, and more complexly integrated over time.

The Hunting-Gathering Band

Hunters and gatherers are "primitive" in the sense that, given their simple technology, they are limited in terms of the amount of energy they can capture from the environment; they neither cultivate crops nor raise animals but depend entirely on food that grows wild. Since they can exert no appreciable control over nature, hunters and gatherers must constantly adjust their lives and behavior to nature's caprices and variations. Although they represent the simplest level of human societal integration, hunters and gatherers participate in very complex ecosystems and relate to nature in varied ways. Some, like the Arctic Eskimo and Yahgan of South America, are almost entirely meat and fish eaters; others eat both meat and vegetable foods. Recent studies suggest that most contemporary hunting-gathering peoples are omnivorous. In fact, most are dependent for their caloric consumption less on hunting than on the various plant foods that they gather. Richard Lee (1969) calculated that the Kung Bushmen, hunter-gatherers of the arid Kalahari desert in southwest Africa, derive only 37 percent of their caloric intake from meat. Most of the calories they consume are obtained from nuts and other vegetable products (cf., Woodburn 1968a).

Environment alone does not stimulate the emergence of hunting-gathering as a way of life; any environment can support peoples of various levels of complexity. We find hunting-gathering peoples in a wide variety of environments—in deserts, tropical rain forests, and in polar ice regions. They derive sustenance from a broad range of resources—they eat fish, berries, insects, toads, buffalo, birds, etc. Since they are found in different environments, eating a variety of animal and vegetable foods, what grounds do we have for classifying them together? If we compare contemporary hunting-gathering peoples we find that most of them live where resources like water, game, and vegetable foods are scattered. The areas in which they are found are also commonly subject to periodic fluctuations in the availability of essential resources. The technology with which they exploit their environments is characteristically simple in the sense that it is almost entirely dependent upon human energy (plus fire). The materials and skills essential to the manufacture of hunting-gathering implements (i.e., to the means of production), furthermore, are those available to all members of society. Given their generally marginal and often unpredictable environments, and *given the technology at their disposal,* many contemporary hunting-gathering peoples are limited in terms of what they can hope to get out of their living space. Another way of putting this is that, given their means of energy capture, the diverse environments in which most contemporary hunter-gatherers are found are generally low in productivity and limited in terms of population carrying capacity. Hunting-gathering bands tend to be small, flexible in composition, and physically mobile—hunters and gatherers move often in search of food and/or other essential resources. Rarely do bands exceed 100 in population and population density is usually well below 1 person per square mile (see Lee and DeVore 1968: 3-20; cf., White 1949). As Julian Steward has pointed out, the *kind* of animals hunted and plants gathered may also have an impact on the size and mobility of a hunting-gathering band. For example, if the main game animals roam in large herds, like bison or carribou, then it is possible and even preferable for hunters to occasionally form larger assemblages and to hunt cooperatively. But if game is of the sort that occurs in small, scattered groups that move within a relatively confined range, then it is better for hunters to live and hunt in relatively smaller groups (Steward 1955: 123-124).

It should be noted that the characteristic nomadism of most hunter-gatherers and the flexible composition of their social groups do not necessarily arise solely from inadequate or unreliable food sources. The Hadza of Africa, for example, live in small and unstable nomadic groups even though they are not required to do so in terms of the availability of food and water (Woodburn 1968a). They apparently move long before shortages emerge. James Woodburn, an anthropologist who spent several years among the Hadza offered the following explanation for their nomadism:

> The Hadza, like many other nomadic people, value movement highly and individuals and groups move to satisfy the slightest whim. Their possessions are so few and so easily carried that movement is no

problem. Indeed people often find it easier to move to the place where a game animal has been killed than to carry the meat back to their camp. The Hadza may move camp to get away from a site where illness has broken out, to obtain raw materials—stone for smoking pipes, wood for arrow shafts, poison for arrows, herbal medicines and so on, to trade, to gamble, to allow the realignment of the huts in a camp after changes in camp composition, to segregate themselves from those with whom they are in conflict, and for many other reasons. People do often move primarily because food and water are less readily available than they would like; and even where some other motive is present, they will of course at the same time try to improve their access to food and water (1968a: 106).

Within the hunting-gathering band reciprocal sharing between families is extensive and expected and often there is sharing between bands as well. Such "generalized reciprocity" (Sahlins 1965) is a hallmark of economy at this level of cultural integration—the necessities of life are freely shared and exchanged without an obvious calculation of balance, without immediate compensation, and even without an overt expression of gratitude in many cases. Sharing and reciprocity are highly adaptive given the limitations of a hunting-gathering technology and the susceptibility of the environments in which such people are often found to periodic fluctuations in the availability of essential resources. If Bushmen bands refused to share water during periods of drought they probably could not survive as a society. And by sharing food, some hunting-gathering peoples are in a sense compensating for a technological inability to store food.

Another characteristic of most contemporary hunting-gathering societies is the absence of a clearly defined and powerful leadership. Especially lacking are individuals with coercive power—with an ability to *force* others to do what they want done. At most we find individuals of influence with respect to various activities. Influence with respect to one activity, however, may not extend to other activities; the best hunter may not be the best singer or dancer. Hunting-gathering bands lack not only a strong and well defined leadership, but they also lack specialization of function. Practically all men and women possess the basic skills appropriate to people of their age and sex. There are no full-time priests, arrow-makers, iron-workers or other specialists of any sort. All adult members of society earn their living in essentially the same way and employ essentially the same means.

In hunting-gathering societies we do not find anything resembling a pecking-order based on physical dominance. As a matter of fact, the common marks of status are generosity and modesty and the reward of status is prestige rather than wealth or the power to coerce others. Another way of saying this is that hunting-gathering society is fundamentally egalitarian. Differences in intelligence, speed, strength, age, sexual prowess, visual acuity, etc., are recognized but society lacks any formal ranking or stratification.* In an egalitarian society there are, as Morton Fried put it, "as many positions of prestige in any given age-sex grade as there are people capable of filling them" (1968: 465). There is no limitation, for example, on the number of "good hunters" in a hunting-gathering band, and indeed we often find customs that operate to preclude the emergence of wide gaps in ability or prestige. In same societies, for example, credit for a hunting kill is given to the man who first saw the animal, who first struck it, or to the individual whose weapon first struck it, rather than to the person who actually killed the animal. We may view such practices as mechanisms (even if unconscious and unintended) that allow credit and prestige for bringing in the game (and access to the game itself) to be spread among all the eligible men in a society.

While specific bands may be identified with particular ranges, localities, or territories, we find that, among contemporary hunting-gathering peoples at least, territories are not exclusively occupied or defended against all outsiders (see, for example, Woodburn 1968a, 1968b). The territory of a band may be closed to strangers and enemies, but it is usually open to friends and allies (who are normally also relatives of one sort or another). Territorial flexibility, like food sharing, is adaptive in that it enables hunters and gatherers to compensate for temporary or periodic variations in the availability of the resources contained within any given range.° When there is a shortage of food for one reason or another, or when water or some other needed resource is temporarily scarce, one can visit and stay with relatives living in a territory where conditions are better.

Thus far we have been discussing the environments in which *contemporary* hunters and gatherers are found. But we should keep in mind that all areas of our globe populated by humans over 10,000 years ago were inhabited by hunters and gatherers, and that this stage of human development accounts for over 90 percent of our existence on earth.* In paleolithic times hunting-gathering bands were not limited, as they are today, to the most marginal and unproductive environments. They lived on the coast of Peru, rich in sea life, in the forests of California, abundant in acorns, and in the temperate areas of Europe and North America where it was also relatively easy to make a living by hunting and gathering. But as superior technologies were discovered and developed, it became possible for some people to extract more food from the same environments and to use that food to underwrite larger, denser populations and more complex forms of social organization. Wherever superior technologies could be applied, hunting-gathering peoples were eventually displaced and, in time, their distribution came to be limited to the relatively inhospitable areas of the world in which we now find so many of them.* If we would understand the forces that shape the way hunting-gathering peoples organize themselves, we must be aware that conditions under which such peoples *now* live may not be the same as those under which their paleolithic predecessors once lived. As Raoul Naroll has observed, "all societies have equally long histories. No present-day human societies are known to preserve unchanged the conditions of *their own ancestors*—much less the conditions of *our* ancestors" (1970: 1242; see also Martin 1969).

There is some disagreement among anthropologists as to whether paleolithic hunters and gatherers were peaceful or combative in terms of their intergroup relations, and the matter is far from resolved. Some scholars play down the importance of fighting among hunting-gathering peoples and stress the fact that, among contemporary hunter-gatherers at least, peacefulness and community "openness" is facilitated by marital alliances contracted between families and between bands. Marital, or "affinal" connections define alliances and reduce the likelihood and intensity of fighting between intermarrying families and groups (Tylor 1889, Mauss 1954, Lévi-Strauss 1949, Sahlins 1963, Fox 1967, Glass and Meggitt 1969). But others suggest that intermarrying groups are not necessarily peaceful and that marital exchange may actually be correlated with high rates of hostility (Mayer 1950, Brown 1964, Hayano 1974). According to one anthropologist, for example, "the direct exchange of women between villages can be considered a *reaction* to warfare rather than a successful *deterrent* to ongoing hostility and future offenses" (Hayano 1974: 289). According to this view marriage may not prevent fighting as much as help terminate it by creating semipermanent alliances.

Commenting on the nature of fighting in hunting-gathering society, one writer has observed that:

> armed conflict between individuals is never totally eliminated but these conflicts lack the common, total-group involvement characteristic of true warfare? Groups like the Andaman Islanders, the Todas, the Western Shoshoni, the Yahgan, and the Mission Indians of California simply lack true equivalents of warfare. As among the Eskimo, members of these groups engage in armed aggression but usually only to avenge particular deaths or personal wrongs. Vengeance parties tend to be small and hostilities are terminated at the first death or serious injury (Harris 1971: 225).

It is interesting to note that when anthropologist, Keith Otterbein (1970b), compared the frequencies of internal and external warfare (i.e., fighting within and between societies) among bands, tribes, chiefdoms, and states (forty-six societies in all) he discovered no significant differences in terms of level of societal complexity. Hunting-gathering bands were found to fight as often as other societies (see also Otterbein and Otterbein 1960).

Using a 50-case sample of hunting-gathering societies, Carol Ember (in press) found that people were involved in fighting in twenty-three out of thirty-four cases at least once in two years and did not seem to fight at all in only three societies! In other words, the cross-cultural evidence suggests that hunting-gathering peoples fight as often as other people. Indeed Elman Service has speculated that hunter-gatherers may once have fought even more than they do now (1962: 49). Competition and open hostility may have been more tolerable in terms of long-term survival when such peoples occupied areas less marginal than those they now live in.

But even if hunters and gatherers fight, and even if they once fought more often than they do now, we have no reason to suppose that they ever lived in closed or exclusive communities or that aggression and hostility were ever more important than cooperation either within or between bands. We should also keep in mind that frequency is not the only aspect of fighting worthy of consideration. Attention should also be given to the nature or quality of warfare and, in this regard, it seems possible to suggest some generalizations of special relevance to hunting-gathering peoples. As M. H. Fried has pointed out (1967: 99-106), people at this cultural level usually spend relatively little time fighting or preparing for war. They do not build fortifications, stockpile supplies or train for battle, and armed encounters tend to be of short duration. The most common military action involves a raid or foray conducted by a few warriors, the conduct of which usually lacks clearly defined command or coordination. In most cases warriors exercise considerable discretion and initiative (cf., Otterbein 1970b).

Some anthropologists have suggested that more common intergroup hostility, combined with the special importance of economic cooperation among males, may have produced a greater propensity for "patrilocality" and "band exogamy" among paleolithic hunters and gatherers than among their contemporary counterparts (see, for example, Service 1962: 66-83; or Steward 1955: 122-142; cf., Martin 1969). At the time of marriage the woman normally left her own band to join that of her husband. Contemporary hunting-gathering bands which are neither exogamous nor patrilocal are sometimes referred to as "composite" bands, and it has been suggested that such bands may represent the relatively recent realignment of unrelated peoples in response to the catastrophic depopulation that resulted from contact with modern civilizations (see Service 1962: 83-107; Steward 1955: 143-150). The merits of these speculations will be discussed later at some length when we consider the possible determinants of different rules of postmarital residence.

The results of recent studies of hunting-gathering peoples require that we reconsider some long-cherished beliefs. It has been commonly assumed, for example, that hunting-gathering peoples live at the fringes of starvation, that they spend all their waking hours looking for food in an effort to avoid starvation, and that they usually die young (see, for example, Steward 1955: 105; and Slater 1959). But in a classic study of the Kung Bushmen, occupants of one of the world's most marginal desert environments, Richard Lee (1969) discovered that these African hunter-gatherers neither die young nor spend all or even most of their time avoiding starvation. His data suggest that hunters and gatherers, especially those living under conditions less marginal than those of the Bushmen, may enjoy more leisure time per capita than people engaged in other subsistence activities. Rice cultivators may actually have to work harder and longer to pay their taxes and/or rents than hunters and gatherers do to collect the food they need. Starvation may be far more familiar to cultivators than to hunter-gatherers (cf., Carneiro 1968b; and Woodburn 1968a, especially page 54).

While food getting was indeed an essential Bushmen activity, Lee found that the major portion of people's time (four to five days a week) was actually spent in other kinds of activities, like resting or visiting. This discovery alone should cause us to take a second look at some popular beliefs about the conditions under which "civilization" first emerged. Some writers have suggested that the emergence of leisure was a stimulus to the thinking, reflection, specialization, and development of arts and writing with which civilization is associated. Leisure, in turn, had to await the discovery of agriculture and animal domestication (i.e., the neolithic). The idea was that agriculture made surplus production possible which in turn made leisure and culture-building possible. Surplus production was needed to feed those individuals who didn't engage in productive activities directly, and whose leisure was supposedly essential for the development of civilization. But, according to Lee's calculations, if the Bushmen chose to work a bit harder, they could produce a caloric surplus (even if they couldn't store it). As it is they already enjoy an enviable amount of leisure yet manifest none of the signs of civilization. It seems clear, then, that while leisure and surplus production may be preconditions for the emergence of complex society, they are not sufficient conditions for the rise of civilization.

Another interesting point that emerged from Lee's study of the Bushmen is that fluctuations in the availability of water more than in the supply of animal or vegetable foods limit group size and determine group movement. Much of Bushmen behavior reflects the fact that they have to exploit resources near water holes or within a reasonable walking distance from them. The size, density, and mobility of any human population may be shaped by, and responsive to, the availability of a variety of needed resources. Leibig's "law of the minimum" (see Odum 1963: 65–66) is as relevant for human behavior as it is for other living organisms—human populations undoubtedly adjust themselves to limitations imposed by essential resources available in minimal supply. Essential resources may well include such diverse items as water, salt, iodine, or even fish and animal poisons in the case of peoples who hunt by means of them (cf., Woodburn 1968a: 106). A hunting-gathering group like the Bushmen, which derives most of its caloric intake from vegetable sources, might very well be limited in size and mobility by the amount of water, or perhaps by the amount of animal protein that is available. If most essential protein is derived from animals, it is conceivable that natural selection will favor groups of a size and mobility that will preclude overhunting animals and ensure a continuous and reliable protein supply. Even assuming that food resources do not constitute the only population limiting factors affecting hunters and gatherers, there can be little doubt that what such peoples have in common, given their technology and environment, is a severely limited population carrying capacity. From this all other social and cultural similarities flow.

The Tribe

By learning to cultivate crops and domesticate animals humankind was able to harness more of the earth's energy (White 1949). Increased control of the environment meant that people could begin to develop more compact and complexly organized social units, assuming of course that they had some reason for doing so. Elman Service has speculated that, at the outset, the process of development mave have consisted of little more than a proliferation and dispersion of essentially similar local groups. Where continued dispersion became restricted by physical or human barriers, however, increasing competition for available resources may have selected for more effective societal integration—for larger and better consolidated societies (Service 1962: 112; cf., Carneiro 1968a). After an initial proliferation of groups, according to Service's speculation, there probably developed a tendency for groups to specialize in function and, as the number and types of groups composing society increased, there also arose a need for some qualitatively different kind of cement to hold them together. A new integrating mechanism eventually did emerge; in addition to bonds of marriage, society also came to be integrated in terms of what Service has called, "pan-tribal sodalities," or nonresidential groups. Some, like clans and lineages, were based on real or presumed descent from a common ancestor. Sodalities of this sort were probably especially common if only because tribal society, like band society, continued to be basically familistic. But some tribal societies have also been integrated in terms of sodalities not based on kinship, like age-grade associations or warrior societies. The Cheyenne of North America had a variety of societies that cross-cut local groups—associations with military, social, and ceremonial functions (see Hoebel 1960), and the Arapaho, neighbors of the Cheyenne achieved tribal integration in terms of age-graded associations. We will have more to say about sodalities in general when we consider descent groups in particular in chapter 8.

Apart from the emergence of integrating sodalities, tribes are very much like band societies. Most relationships are similarly expressed in terms of kinship and, like bands, tribes are essentially egalitarian—differences of status do not depend upon relative wealth or upon control of needed resources. In neither bands nor tribes do we find political, economic, or religious speculation. There are no "chiefs" in the sense of individuals who possess the abiding power to enforce decisions and what leadership there is normally depends upon the prestige that attaches to proficiency, wisdom, or age. As in band society, no local group enjoys predominant influence or control over the total unit. In band and tribal society the local or residential units that comprise society are similar; they are essentially autonomous in a political sense and self-sufficient in an economic sense. Because the local units are relatively independent, tribal integration tends to be rather fragile. A presumably less volatile form of societal integration emerged as local groups became specialized and interdependent.

Chiefdoms

In contrast to tribes and bands, chiefdoms are characteristically *ranked* societies, which is to say that there are significant differences between individuals and/or groups in terms of political influence, authority, and prestige. As M. Fried put it, "the rank society is characterized by having fewer positions of valued status than individuals capable of handling them" (1968: 466; see also 1957: 23–24; and 1967: 109–184). It is in chiefdoms that we discover truly authoritative individuals.

The economies of bands and tribes also differ in important ways from those of chiefdoms. Chiefdoms are not only capable of producing sufficient food to support larger and more dense populations, but they have usually developed means for storing food. Still more important, we find that most chiefdoms derive their subsistence from relatively diverse environments. Diversity makes it possible to avoid over-exploitation of any single resource and, even if environmental catastrophies occur, a society that exploits a broad range of resources will enjoy greater security than one which depends on a narrower range of resources. A diverse diet is also likely to be a relatively balanced one. For these reasons it is in the best interest of any society to extend itself over an area which includes as many different resources as possible. There are two ways in which this can be accomplished—one way is to conquer territories that contain coveted resources; another is by establishing trade with societies that control resources not available at home. Both solutions (and they are by no means mutually exclusive) favor establishment of a relatively centralized redistributive social, political, and economic system, from which many other diagnostic features of the chiefdom derive. In chiefdoms redistribution replaces generalized reciprocity as the heart of economy and at the hub of the redistributive system is the "chief."

Among the Trobriand Islanders of Melanesia, for example, men contribute a large part of their yam harvests to their sisters' households and receive comparable contributions from their brothers-in-law. Since village and district chiefs are usually polygymous (i.e., they have more than one wife at a time), the number of yams they receive is greater than that received by ordinary, monogamous men and a chief's storehouses are necessarily larger. But the fact that a Trobriand chief accumulates greater stockpiles of yams does not mean that he can dispose of them as he pleases. To the contrary, every chief has certain obligations that do not bear as heavily upon ordinary men. A chief is expected to underwrite feasts and ceremonies to which all his many in-laws are invited, and his yams also constitute a kind of public reserve—an insurance against famine. In short, the Trobriand chief functions as a custodian of certain basic resources. Enacting his chiefly role greatly adds to his prestige and authority, but the possession of yams in great abundance in no significant way adds to his personal well-being or wealth. Unlike money, yams have very limited uses. They are mainly eaten and it is not likely that any chief or chiefly family, no matter what their appetite, could consume all the yams that a chief acquires (see Malinowski 1922; or Service 1971: 229–49).

The nature and function of chiefly status can also be illustrated by reference to Indians of the American northwest coast. Among the Nootka of British Columbia, for example, individuals, families, and certain descent group segments are ranked and the hierarchy that results is also evident in the economic system in the sense that stewardship of certain critical resources, like hunting and fishing grounds, is vested in individuals ranked high in the social system. Elman Service described the Nootka system as follows:

> The various grades of chiefs have various amounts of territory over which they act as executives for lesser kinsmen. Those who use the resources formally acknowledge the positions by paying sorts of tributes, such as the first fruits of the salmon catch or berry-picking, certain choice parts of sea mammals killed, blankets, furs, and so on. Many economic products are acquired by the chief according to strict and complicated custom, but quantities of goods are also given

to the chief more freely, when there is a surplus beyond the donor's subsistence needs. The chief has no means to enforce these divisions of the products, of course, . . . Furthermore, these gifts do not function particularly to increase personal wealth which the chief might consume, for it is understood that he will later give away a comparable amount of goods in a great feast or potlatch. The chief's function is to redistribute goods. . . ." (1971: 216–217).

One of the major purposes of the "potlatch" among northwest coast Indians is to preserve and validate rank, but the custom also has important economic consequences. Potlatching involves a ceremonial and highly competitive redistribution of surplus goods, the effect of which may be to compensate for local shortages resulting from seasonal fluctuations in the availability of resources. In their studies of northwest coast Indians, P. Vayda and W. Suttles have both demonstrated how the potlatch may have functioned to redistribute goods within and between communities in such a way as to enhance the survival potentialities of the entire population (see Suttles 1960, and Vayda 1968).

The system of redistribution and the ranked social hierarchy that characterize a chiefdom seem to reinforce each other; in some contexts social inequality may actually constitute a trait selected for by the environment and technology. Ranking and redistribution may be especially adaptive where the danger of localized food shortages exist. Most chiefdoms are found in territories that are capable, given suitable redistributive mechanisms, of supporting larger and more dense populations than are usually found in bands or tribes. The higher population carrying capacity made possible by more productive and more diverse environments undoubtedly accounts for the other social and political differences that distinguish tribes and chiefdoms. And yet, the fact that there are parts of the world where chiefdoms have not emerged despite the presence of diverse and potentially highly productive environments suggests that some catalyst may be necessary to inspire realization of environmental and technological potentialities.[6]

The State

Chiefdoms are ranked societies but, in their archetypical form, there is neither exploitative economic power nor genuine political power; there is no locus of power that can exercise a monopoly over the use of force. The function of a chief is to distribute and give away rather than to consume, and he performs his redistributive role in the absence of genuine coercive power. It is the emergence in society of differential access to the means and products of production, and it is the rise of true coercive power, that signal the presence of a new level of societal integration—the state.

As Morton Fried pointed out (1967: 189), stratification is the setting in which "exploitation" is born, and the emergence of stratification in society was a prelude to the emergence of the state. It was from stratification that all other diagnostic features of the state emerged. Chiefdoms, being ranked societies, operate on the principle of different privilege, status, and prestige for individuals with similar abilities, but a prestigious status does not necessarily involve or imply economic and political power. In truly stratified societies, on the other hand, some members of society have free access to the means of production and its fruits while others have restricted access to the same resources (Fried 1968: 470; 1957: 24; and 1967: 185–242). Certain individuals or groups "own" these resources while other individuals or groups may make use of them only under certain conditions: they may purchase access to them with their labor or with part of the product of their labor. The order of stratification may be based upon a hierarchy of relatively open or of relatively closed "classes," the latter usually being referred to as "castes." Harris described the difference between the two kinds of stratification in the following terms:

> Classes differ greatly in the manner in which membership is established and in the rate at which membership changes. When class membership is established exclusively through hereditary ascription —through the inheritance of durable power in the form of money, property, or some other form of wealth—there is necessarily a low rate of mobility in or out. Such a class is spoken of as being "closed" (it is also sometimes referred to as being a *caste* or as being "caste-like," . . .). The ruling classes of the Oriental despotic states, the nobility of the seventeenth-century Europe, the highest echelons of contemporary super millionaire elites in the United States are examples of superordinate closed classes (1971: 430).

Castes, or relatively closed classes, are usually endogamous and the consequence of confining marriage to members of the same group is, as Harris notes, the consolidation, concentration, and perpetuation of control over the means and products of production (1971: 430).

It is not likely that appeals to common kinship alone would be sufficient to keep the disadvantaged in their place in a growing, stratified population, especially if that population contained a disproportionate number of unrelated people. Under such circumstances a new kind of societal integration is necessary—one that can cut across kin and local groups to integrate people on a territorial basis. In addition, a new kind of power is necessary to bolster the order of stratification, and it is this locus of coercive power that we usually refer to as the "state." As Fried put it, it is the task of maintaining general social order that stands at the heart of the development of the state. And at the heart of the problem of maintaining general order is the need to defend the central order of stratification—the differentiation of categories of population in terms of access to basic resources. . . . Every state known to history has had a physical apparatus for removing or otherwise dealing with those who failed to get the message (1967: 230–231; see also 1968).

Associated with the emergence of state institutions is the emergence of taxation and law. Taxation is necessary to support the developing bureaucracy and law, or rules "enforced by sanctions administered by a determinate locus of power" (Fried 1967: 20), is required to define rights and privileges.

Under what conditions do states emerge? In most cases known to us from history the move to the state was accomplished through a kind of pulling process—non-state peoples were inspired, engulfed, or conquered by state organized ones. So most of the states that are known to us are what Fried has called "secondary" states in the sense that they are based upon a preexisting model. But where and under what circumstances did the world's first, or "pristine" states emerge? In the absence of a model, what conditions might have stimulated the emergence of stratification and the concentration of power, and what factors might have influenced the kind of state that emerged? These are questions that have inspired many learned treatises and speculations, but they are also questions for which we are still without final and definitive answers.

On the Sources of Societal Transformation

Everyone seems to agree that in the general development of humankind the emergence of complex forms of society was, in most instances, related to the greater population carrying capacity of agriculture and animal domestication. Domestication provided greater potentialities for population growth, and population growth in some cases necessitated more complex forms of organization. We are still not sure if population expanded on the heels of the discovery of domestication, or if domestication developed in response to population growth, or if, as seems likely, there was some kind of complex feedback between population growth and domestication (cf., Spooner 1972). Nor do we completely understand why population growth led to increasing societal complexity in some cases but not in others. Why did some people realize their potentialities for development while others did not?

As was observed earlier, there is reason to believe that hunting-gathering is not necessarily associated with either starvation or excessive physical exertion. If this mode of subsistence is so satisfactory, why then did most of humankind eventually abandon it in favor of domestication? Although the circumstances of this transition have been much discussed, they are still poorly understood. One especially interesting and promising speculation has been proposed by Robert Carneiro (1968b). In calculating the margin of productivity between hunting and simple horticultural peoples of the Amazon Basin, Carneiro found little significant difference. He therefore suggested that "factors other than productivity" alone may well have inspired the *initial* acceptance of agriculture (1968b: 159). Carneiro suggested that peoples living near concentrated sources of protein (e.g., fishabundant major rivers) may have been more inclined to make the transition to agriculture than those whose sources of protein were more mobile or scattered (e.g., animals of various sorts). Hunting did not permit the degree of sedentariness and population concentration that fishing did, and sedentariness may therefore have been the factor that especially favored the development and elaboration of horticulture. °

Most anthropologists have assumed that the population expansion that occurred during the neolithic period was a direct and necessary consequence of an increased capacity for food production. It is simply assumed that population grew at an unprecedented rate because domestication increased the food supply, ensured a more stable supply of food, and presumably improved nutrition. But as Robert Sussman recently noted (1972), even if this is so we are still uncertain as to how the potentiality for population growth was translated into reality. Was growth in numbers the result of decreasing mortality rates, longer life expectancy, or of more favorable fertility performance? Sussman suggests that there may actually have been a rise in mortality rates during the neolithic since epidemic diseases more easily spread in compact, settled communities (1972: 258). Why then did world population increase so precipitously with the discovery of domestication? On the basis of what is known of nonhuman primates, Sussman speculates that once human groups became sedentary (a condition that usually presupposes domestication), child-spacing mechanisms may have been less essential: ₊

> In hunting and gathering populations, in which it is necessary to move constantly in order to obtain food, there will be limits on the number of children a woman can rear in her lifetime. If a woman must transport a child until it can walk far and fast enough to keep up with the group, she is definitely limited in the number of children she can support at any one time (1972: 259).

In other words, it might have been the development of sedentary living patterns rather than the domestication of plants and animals per se that resulted in the remarkable population increase that took place during the neolithic period—in short, "with the burden of child transport relieved, social spacing mechanisms became less necessary" (Sussman 1972: 259). But whatever the mechanism, it is certain that world population did dramatically increase during the neolithic period precipitating, in *some* places, the emergence of more complex forms of social and political organization.

There does not appear to be some inevitable or uniform way in which people everywhere respond to the social and political potentialities of a commitment to agriculture. Much seems to depend on the *kind* of agriculture to which they commit themselves which is in turn related to the sort of social and physical environment in which they find themselves. An example of the significance of differing patterns of domestication is provided by a comparison of tropical slash-and-burn (or swidden) cultivation with the cultivation of rice paddies. As Clifford Geertz (1963) points out, tropical soils are relatively infertile (i.e., low in nutrient content) due to the leaching effects of heavy rainfall. The decomposition of organic materials and the recycling of nutrients to living organisms must be very fast under such conditions. The recycling process in tropical swiddens is hastened by human intervention—people cut and burn the forest cover. No matter how efficiently this is done, however, there is unavoidably some loss of nutrients and energy—some nitrogen goes up in smoke and some ash is washed away by the rains before it can be recycled. A major consequence of this technological inefficiency is that there will eventually be a drop in fertility and yield if a field is slashed-and-burned over and over without an occasional period of fallow.

Although leaching also renders paddy soils relatively infertile, nutrients are constantly replenished with the introduction of irrigation water and, as a result, the paddy can be cultivated year after year with virtually undiminished yield. Certain social consequences follow from solving the nutrient problem in this particular way. For one thing, irrigation involves special skills and technical ability. It also requires heavy investment in capital equipment (in canals, diversions, dams, dikes, tunnels, and the like), as well as in labor. But given such inputs, a paddy can be made to produce yields sufficient to support a relatively dense population. According to Geertz:

> This complex of systemic characteristics—settled stability, "medium" rather than "substratum" nutrition, technical complexity and significant overhead labor investment—produce in turn what is perhaps the sociologically most critical feature of wet-rice agriculture: its marked tendency (and ability) to respond to a rising population through intensification; that is, through absorbing increased numbers of cultivators on a unit of cultivated land. Such a course is largely precluded

to swidden farmers, at least under traditional conditions, because of the precarious equilibrium of the shifting regime. If their population increases they must, before long, spread out more widely over the countryside in order to bring more land under cultivation (1963: 32).

Where tropical swiddens are overexploited, yields dwindle and the ecosystem itself changes. Where swidden cultivators increase in number, therefore, they must eventually spread themselves out in space (if this is possible) to avoid overtaxing existing fields. Paddy cultivators, on the other hand, have the option of working existing fields more intensively and efficiently; even if resulting increments of yield are not sufficient to prevent starvation, increasing population does not lead to degradation of the paddy. Geertz also points out that because of the considerable investment of capital and energy made in their waterworks, paddy cultivators usually prefer to respond to increasing demands by squeezing a bit more out of existing fields rather than by starting new ones elsewhere, and paddy cultivation therefore tends to encourage a kind of agricultural "involution," or "introversion."

Noting the apparently limited population carrying capacity of tropical swiddens, some scholars (e.g., Meggers 1954 and 1960) have concluded that the first civilizations probably could not have emerged on the basis of this form of cultivation. There is reason to believe, however, that the population carrying capacity of swiddening is often underestimated. Robert Carneiro (1968a; cf., 1970) has demonstrated that while communities of the Kuikuru, a slash-and-burn people of the Amazon basin, normally range between 50 and 150 in population their technology could have provided, without soil depletion, sufficient caloric support for larger and more sedentary communities. Carneiro suggests that the Kuikuru did not form such communities mainly because land was abundant, movement was relatively simple, and there were no political leaders capable of inhibiting or preventing community fission.

Community fission served to short-circuit both the rising interpersonal tensions of growing communities and the ultimate dangers of soil depletion. Carneiro's conclusion with regard to the nature of Kuikuru communities is of particular interest and relevance:

> Production of a true food surplus is not a matter of agricultural technology alone. The presence of certain additional factors—economic incentives or political compulsion—appears to be required before a people's economic system can be made to generate the food surplus which is an inherent potential of almost every agricultural society (1968a: 137; cf., 1970).

Some such catalyst was probably present in Ceylon, on the Malabar coast of India, in Cambodia, in Java and Sumatra, in Tahiti, and in

Hawaii. In all of these places transition to the state may have initially been predicated on some form of slash-and-burn cultivation. What sort of catalysts might dispose people to generate sufficient food resources to support a denser, more complexly integrated population? Carneiro suggests one possibility when he proposes that swidden cultivators are likely to farm more intensively to support larger and more complexly organized societies when they find themselves in circumscribed areas—in situations where there is no longer a possibility for expansion. The limits may be topographic (e.g., mountains or deserts) or human (e.g., the presence of hostile neighbors). The agricultural intensification that results when population growth takes place in confined spaces produces competition for available resources, and competition selects for more effective organization. It thus leads to firmer political integration, occupational specialization, and to the emergence of classes based on differential access to the means of production. It leads, ultimately, to the state.

There may be other factors that contribute to agricultural intensification or to increasing organizational complexity. Even where land is abundant, for example, the menace of hostile populations alone might conceivably inspire a shift to forms of cultivation that would reduce the area of fields needed to support a given population. If sources of water were available, irrigation would provide one way to support a large and concentrated population without the necessity of having to cultivate fields located too far from protective walls and fortifications. An initial commitment to modest forms of irrigation might initially inspire the emergence of ranked chiefdoms in which the chief's role would be to control irrigation and drainage facilities (see Fried 1968: 469; and 1967: 183), but more complicated systems of irrigation would ultimately require even more complex forms of societal integration (i.e., states).

Julian Steward has suggested yet another setting that might be conducive to state formation. "Microterritorial specialization," like irrigation, can create a need for centralized coordination and concentrated power, especially where the production and redistribution of surpluses must be forced. States are unlikely to develop, says Steward, where all people exploit a variety of resources and there is no specialization as between particular groups. States are more likely to emerge, however, where different territorial groups draw upon different microenvironmental resources (i.e., where there is microterritorial specialization). But could not the redistribution of resources as between microterritories be handled in other ways—through tribal-like trade, or on the basis of chiefly redistribution networks, for example? Under what circumstances would it be necessary to generate a determinant locus of power (a state)? Inherent in Steward's discussion is the assumption that where population is large and microterritories numerous, exchange must sometimes be *forced*. Some people have to be pressed to produce more than they themselves require, and trade may become so complicated as to require a specialized staff with powers of coercion to carry it out.* As Steward put it,

> Agriculture became a factor in state evolution not because it gave men access to a new source of energy external to man himself but because, when additional factors were present, it gave certain classes of men access to the energy of other men. These additional factors include: many varieties of crops, microterritorial specialization, exchange of produce, and irrigation. In various combinations, these factors required a regulatory institution or class . . . (1970: 220).

As we have seen, then, commitment to agriculture leads to increasingly complex social and political forms only under certain circumstances, and the tentative nature of our speculations thus far should make it clear that there is still much to be learned about the kinds of variables that inspire people to realize their organizational potentialities. Even where this potential has been realized there are differences in the end result. States have been established on the basis of many forms of cultivation but there is reason to believe that different forms of agriculture may predispose people to different kinds of states.* The social historian, Karl Wittfogel (1957 and 1968), has been especially interested in the relationship between differing forms of cultivation and kinds of state organization.

According to Wittfogel, there are basically two varieties of agriculture —rainfall dependent and irrigation dependent—and the social, political, and economic consequences of each are quite different. Complex irrigation and drainage facilities require management; water has to be allocated and controlled in such a way as to minimize competition and prevent conflict. Irrigation technology requires the cultivation of a high degree of technical and managerial expertise and presupposes an ability to call up, organize, and supervise large labor forces. Those who manage, organize, and defend irrigation facilities must be able to enforce their demands and exactions. In addition, cultivators must be persuaded (by force if necessary) to generate sufficient food to maintain the managerial, logistical, military, and other establishment agencies required by the irrigation system. In short, a commitment to extensive irrigation agriculture requires a state apparatus (if one does not already exist). In addition, it requires a highly centralized state in which all coordination and power ultimately emanate from the center. Other foci of power which might succeed in diverting revenues from the center must be eliminated or at least kept well in check since such diversion could seriously impair the state's ability to fulfill its basic function, which is to maintain, manage, and protect the irrigation system. The characteristic "despotic" centralism of hydraulic ("oriental") states, and even their cyclic dynastic patterns, are attributed, by Wittfogel, to the inevitable demands of the irrigation network.

In less arid regions, where cultivation can be predicated upon rainfall, there is no comparable need for absolute centralized control over either resources or manpower and, according to Wittfogel, such regions are the breeding grounds for a different kind of state—one comprised of a loose federation of relatively independent and autonomous "feudal" landlords. In such states there are no central economic functions which might give the ruler and his court an ability to suppress competitive sources of power.

Wittfogel proposes that the developmental trajectories of hydraulic and feudal states are also quite distinct. The development of capitalism and socialism that took place in feudal Europe, for example, could not occur (at least indigenously) in the context of a hydraulic state. In the feudal setting, according to Wittfogel,

> the transition to capitalism occurred in cities, which knew how to make themselves independent by a chain of more or less political aggressive movements. The surplus from handicraft and commercial activity remained in the hands of the bourgeois class, under whose control it grew. The accumulation of capital was thus possible politically as well as economically; the surplus was not taxed away, confiscated, or taken away as a pseudo-loan. The industrial productive powers could be developed as well, without negatively touching the agricultural hinterland, in whose urban centers the new development took place; and the absolute central power had to encourage industrial progress all the more eagerly, since here, in contrast to the feudally-controlled villages, it expected additional income and power for the court and its administration (1968: 197).

Unlike its feudal counterpart, the hydraulic state once formed is a socio-cultural deadend, according to Wittfogel. Dynasties may rise and fall, but each version of despotic centralism essentially reproduces its predecessor. It must do so because the requirements of irrigation remain basically the same. Since the state continues to dominate all revenues and their sources, industrial capitalism can take no root.

In conclusion, the discovery of domestication certainly played a key role in the transition of humankind from simple hunting-gathering bands to tribes, chiefdoms, and to various forms of the state. Although it is clear that we still have much to learn about the particular causes of social transformation, the increasing complexity of society in general, and of societies in particular, was undoubtedly the product of a complex interplay between human organisms, technology, and environment. Having traced the general line of human societal development, and having pointed to some of the factors that may have influenced and channeled societal transformation, let us now turn our attention to particular aspects of human kinship and social organization. We will especially focus on variations in form and consider the variables that may be influential in producing them.

3

Incest Regulations

All human societies formulate rules and regulations to govern and restrict sexual relations between certain kinds of relatives; "incestuous" relations are those which violate such "taboos." Some years ago, G. P. Murdock (1949: 284–313) compared incest regulations in 250 societies and discovered certain common features. For one thing, sexual relations are everywhere prohibited between persons of opposite sex within the nuclear family (parents and children), excepting of course between a husband and wife. Siblings have been allowed to violate this restriction in a few societies (e.g., in precontact Incan and Hawaiian society as well as in ancient Egypt), but suspension of the usual prohibition in these cases was not made for the general public; it was mainly limited to royal families (see Goggin and Sturtevant 1964). Because incest taboos discourage sexual relations among primary relatives everywhere, conjugal families cannot be independent or self-sufficient when it comes to the selection of mates. The consequence of prohibiting sexual relations among primary relatives, therefore, is that marriage invariably involves the establishment of some connection between different conjugal units. ₆

Another discovery made by Murdock was that all societies also prohibit sexual intercourse with some relatives outside the nuclear family; they do not all rule out the *same* relatives, however. Some Chinese consider it desirable for a man to marry (and therefore to have sexual relations with) his maternal cross cousin (MoBrDa); he cannot marry any other cousin even though they are biologically no closer to him than his MoBrDa. In our own society it would be unthinkable for a man to marry his paternal aunt (FaSi) or his maternal aunt (MoSi). Among the Marquesans of Polynesia and the Yaruro of Venezuela, however, the paternal aunt is a potential spouse; the maternal aunt is allowed among the Osset of the Caucasus and among the Sema of Burma. In some societies (e.g., Lakher, Menta-weians, Edo, and Minangkabau) siblings may marry if they share only one parent. In short, while incest regulations everywhere extend beyond the nuclear family, the manner in which they do varies considerably. Beyond the nuclear family incest taboos bear no direct relationship to nearness of biological relationship.

Murdock's cross-cultural comparison revealed a tendency to extend incest taboos to all relatives referred to by a kinship term appropriate to a primary relative (i.e., to a parent, sibling, or child). If a certain woman is referred to as "sister," for example, she is likely to be sexually taboo even if she is not a biological sister. One anthropologist has personally witnessed a ceremony intended to expiate an act of sibling incest among the Mnong Gar of Vietnam (Condominas 1973: 211–226). The offending "brother" and "sister" in this instance were required to taste the excrement of pig and dog despite the fact that their actual relationship was based upon a common ancestor fifteen generations removed! On the other hand, Murdock also found that incest taboos apply with diminished intensity to kinsmen outside the nuclear family even if they are referred to by kinship terms appropriate to primary relatives. If a first cousin is referred to as "sister," for example, sexual relations with her are usually considered to be a less serious violation of incest taboos than sexual intercourse with a biological sister. Murdock's comparison indicated, however, that violation of an incest taboo is usually considered more serious than any other kind of sexual offense, including adultery and violation of menstrual restrictions.

Few anthropologists deny the universality of incest regulations in human society but there is considerable disagreement about how incest taboos first got started, about the functions they perform, and over why they do not apply to the same relatives in all societies. It is to such questions that we now turn.

Incest, Infanticide, and the Meaning of Blood

During the nineteenth and early twentieth centuries some social philosophers suggested a connection between incest regulation and certain other social customs and primitive beliefs. Some, for example, proposed a relationship between incest taboos and female infanticide (e.g., John Lubbock, Herbert Spencer, and John McLennan). The connection was postulated by John McLennan (1865), for example, on the assumption that female infanticide was commonly practiced in early human society to enhance fighting efficiency in the face of frequent and recurrent interband conflict. Female infanticide presumably enhanced fighting efficiency by reducing the number of nonfighters that had to be supported. But female infanticide supposedly also had the effect of reducing the number of potential mates available in any group, making it necessary for men to find their mates in other groups. In some cases women had to be obtained by capture from groups that were also short of females. Although the practice of infanticide was later abandoned, and even where the intensity of fighting decreased, the custom of marrying out of one's local group continued in force, and incest regulation supposedly functioned to bolster this exogamic commitment. As a matter of fact there is some cross-cultural support for the belief that female infanticide is not uncommon among hunter-gatherers; William Divale has provided evidence that female infanticide and blood-revenge warfare and feuding are interrelated and effective in regulating population growth among such peoples (1972). Nevertheless there are several problems with McLennan's speculation. For one thing, if sexual relations between siblings was unlikely in paleolithic times because of extensive female infanticide, why then should it have been necessary to create a taboo to enjoin them? And why should such a taboo have been maintained once the practice of infanticide had been abandoned? Furthermore, how are we to account in terms of female infanticide for the universal taboo against sexual relations between parent and child?

Other scholars have suggested a connection between the universality of incest regulation and certain supposedly universal beliefs. Émile Durkheim suggested, for example, that even the earliest humans must have been aware that loss of blood leads to loss of life—that there is a profound connection between blood and life force (1898). A vivid illustration of this belief is provided in the writings of the ancient Hebrews:

> And the Lord said unto Cain: "Where is Abel thy brother?" And he said: "I know not; am I my brother's keeper?" And He said: "What hast thou done? The voice of thy brother's blood crieth unto Me from the ground. And now cursed art thou from the ground, which hath opened her mouth to receive thy brother's blood from thy hand" *(Genesis* 4: 9–11).

If early humans appreciated the connection between blood and life, reasoned Durkheim, they must also have concluded that one deprives a person of life in proportion to the amount of blood spilled and, for this reason, early people may have been reluctant to shed the blood of close relatives. Since sexual relations may initially involve some loss of blood, early humankind may have preferred to discomfort nonrelatives in this connection. Interesting though this line of reasoning may be, it is flawed by the fact that sexual relations do not invariably involve the shedding of blood and, in many societies, intentional and controlled bleeding is even considered to have curative value.

Psychological Foundations of Incest Regulation

Some scholars have preferred to attribute the persistence and/or initial emergence of incest regulation in human society to supposedly universal psychological processes. Probably most familiar is the notion that primary relatives have a natural propensity for sexual relations—an attraction that must be controlled for the good of familial and societal survival. The most famous proponent of this theory, Sigmund Freud, speculated on the origins of incest regulation in his book, *Totem and Taboo* (1931), where he proposed the following sequence of events:

During the earliest stages of human existence, society probably consisted of very small, father-dominated groups. In each, the father monopolized all females (his wives and daughters) and drove his sons from the group as they approached sexual maturity. "One day," wrote Freud, "the expelled brothers joined forces, slew and ate the father, and thus put an end to the father horde. Together they dared and accomplished what would have remained impossible for them singly" (1931: 247). Having murdered and eaten their father, however, the brothers experienced profound remorse and guilt and, for this reason, they agreed *not* to divide up their father's females and to seek their own mates elsewhere. Somehow this landmark decision was passed from generation to generation.

There is absolutely no evidence that things actually happened the way Freud has proposed; even many nonhuman primate groups lack a dominant male who actively prevents younger males from copulating with available females. And even if Freud's reconstruction of early group life were true, why should patricide have generated guilt; and even if the sons had experienced guilt why should they have chosen to assuage their guilt by renouncing the females? Even assuming that guilt led them to make this peculiar sacrifice, by means of what mechanism was their renunciation transmitted from one generation to the next?

According to another version of the psychological approach to incest, taboos arise not in response to a natural attraction between primary relatives, but rather in response to an aversion for sexual relations with such relatives; an antipathy that is either instinctive or which develops when normal individuals are brought up together. In *Primitive Society*, for example, Robert Lowie wrote:

It is not the function of the ethnologist but of the biologist and psychologist to explain why man has so deep-rooted a horror of incest, though personally I accept Hobhouse's view that the sentiment is instinctive (1961: 15).

While he embraced the view that incest regulation is the result of an instinctive aversion for sexual relations between members of the nuclear family, Lowie believed that incest taboos are extended to other relatives for noninstinctive (conventional) reasons, and that this accounts for the variation from society to society (1961: 15; cf., White 1949: 304).

Edward Westermarck, undoubtedly the best known proponent of an aversion hypothesis, believed that an emotional resistance to sexual relations results from childhood association: there is something about being brought up and socialized together that dampens sexual interest (1894). On the basis of ethnographic data collected in northern Taiwan, Arthur Wolf (1966, 1968, 1970a) has recently rekindled interest in Westermarck's hypothesis. Wolf describes a form of marriage (sim-pua marriage) in which a bride enters her future husband's home as an adopted infant; the bride and groom are raised as members of the same family (i.e., as siblings) and experience a prolonged period of intimate association. He proposes that if Westermarck's theory is correct, relationships created by this form of marriage should be less satisfactory than those created by more prestigious forms in which the conjugal union is not preceded by a period of prolonged childhood association. In fact, written household registers reveal that in the area studied sixteen out of eighteen sim-pua betrothals were consummated prior to 1910. However, when opportunities for occupational and physical mobility increased from 1910 to 1930, only two out of seventeen such betrothals eventually resulted in marriage. Wolf also discovered that men who marry sim-pua are more likely to frequent prostitutes than those who marry in the standard fashion and that sim-pua wives are more prone to adulterous relationships than other wives (1966). What is it about early domestic association that might produce an antipathy for marriage and sexual relations? According to Wolf,

the socialization process inevitably involves a good deal of punishment and pain, and children who are socialized together must come to associate one another with this experience (1966: 892).

The fact that sim-pua marriages dropped off after 1910 does not necessarily reflect an underlying aversion for sexual relations. Perhaps it was the challenge of new opportunities rather than an aversion for old ones that inspired the decline. The drop could be a function of increasing opportunity to cultivate romantic relationships with a wider range of potential mates. Wolf indicates that young people in the region were commonly encouraged to marry sim-pua before 1910, but there can be no doubt that young people in northern Taiwan shared with other Chinese the conviction that sexual unions of this sort are less desirable and less prestigious than those resulting from other marriage forms (see Wolf 1966: 887). The fact that so many sim-pua betrothals eventually resulted in marriage before 1910 would seem to suggest that even if sexual aversion resulted from common socialization, it did not stand in the way of marriage. Since sim-pua marriages are rare in most areas of China, moreover, their unusual frequency in northern Taiwan before 1910 calls for some explanation.

In the course of studying marriage patterns in Israeli collectives *(kibbutzim)*, Melford Spiro (1958) and Yonina Talmon (1964) found that young people brought up together by a common staff of nurses and teachers tend to avoid marriage and sexual relations despite the fact that they are not related and even though they are not discouraged from marrying. These findings too would seem to provide support for the Westermarck hypothesis. However, if people brought up together develop a pattern of sexual avoidance is it the result of common socialization as Westermarck and Wolf have suggested or is it because they have been enjoined from having sexual relations? If they have been taught to avoid sexual relations then we must ask *why* they should have been so instructed. Furthermore it is significant that members of the same peer group on the Israeli *kibbutz*, unlike potential participants in a sim-pua marriage, *do* manifest considerable sexual interest in each other as children. Continued interest is intentionally discouraged as children approach puberty and adolescence, when sexual relations are generally considered frivolous and inappropriate.

In both the Chinese and Israeli cases disinterest in sexual relations on the part of individuals brought up together could be the result of both avoidance training and of a desire to experience something (and someone) new and exciting. What must be accounted for is the presence of avoidance training in both instances; why should it be necessary to discourage sexual relations that people either want (according to the Freudian theory) or do not want (according to Westermarck)? There is another problem inherent in any psychological interpretation of incest regulation. As David Aberle et al. observed some years ago:

> With a little ingenuity, virtually any universal phenomenon can be explained by, or be used to explain the existence of, any other universal phenomenon in the realm under discussion. There are no criteria save aesthetics and logical consistency for choosing among theories, since there is no possibility of demonstrating that A varies from B, if both A and B are universally and invariably present (1963: 254).

The Sociological Basis of Incest Regulation

Many anthropologists have been inclined to the view that sexual relations within the family must be discouraged for the sake of intrafamilial
or interfamilial harmony (or for both reasons). Prohibiting sexual relations within the family prevents disruptive sexual competition within that
vital social unit and, by requiring people to find mates in other families,
incest regulation promotes interfamilial alliances and social solidarity.
Bronislaw Malinowski emphasized the contribution of incest regulation
to familial harmony:

> If erotic passions were allowed to invade the precincts of the home
> it would not merely establish jealousies and competitive elements
> and disorganize the family but it would also subvert the most funda-
> mental bonds of kinship on which the further development of all
> social relations is based (1931: 630).

And Brenda Seligman, in a similar vein, suggested that sexual relations
between parents and children would ultimately weaken the authority of
the former and thus undermine familial solidarity and jeopardize encul-
turation (1929: 243–45). But there is good reason to question the validity
of these assumptions. For one thing, members of the same family *do*
share sexual partners in a number of ethnographically described societies.
In Tibet, for example, brothers and even father and son may share a
spouse (so long as she is not the son's biological mother); in other societies
sisters or even a mother and daughter may be married to the same man
(if he is not the daughter's biological father). It has certainly not been
conclusively established that the sharing of sexual favors by members of
the same family inevitably leads to disruption and family disintegration.
Furthermore the introduction of an outsider at the time of marriage can
also generate considerable strain on family harmony; as a matter of fact
the Chinese often justify sim-pua arrangements on the grounds that an
adopted sister who is brought up with her future husband and mother-in-
law makes fewer waves than a bride brought into a family at the time of
marriage. It is possible that only *unregulated* sexual relations among
family members would really be disruptive; and incest taboos are not
the only conceivable way to regulate sexual relations although it is clearly
the method that has been adopted in virtually all societies. Sexual access
within the family could also be institutionalized and regulated by stipu-
lating, in advance, the time, place, and rate of access to be enjoyed by
each member of the family with respect to every other member.

Regulating sexual competition within the family by means of posted schedules and rosters or in terms of phases of the moon would certainly reduce intrafamilial competition and disharmony, but it would not encourage the sort of interfamilial alliances that result when individuals are required to find mates outside their own families. By establishing bonds of marriage between families, then, the incest taboo contributes not only to intrafamilial harmony, but also to interfamilial harmony. When it comes to exploiting the environment or waging war, cooperation among families can confer a definite advantage and, as Tylor long ago speculated, "again and again in the world's history, savage tribes must have had plainly before their minds the simple practical alternative between marrying-out and being killed out" (1889: 267). By widening the sphere of interaction and cooperation, an exchange of spouses between families confers demographic and economic benefits as well as military advantages. As Marvin Harris recently observed,

> the first consequence of this interaction is a pooling of the reproductive and sexual potentials of the constituent units. All the subgroups benefit reproductively since imbalances in the number of males and females produced by momentarily unfavorable birth and death rates can be evened out and demographic crises, which might prove fatal to isolated groups, can be overcome (1971: 296–97).

Harris also noted that marriage increases the productive potential of intermarrying families (and therefore the upper limits of group size) by permitting them to exploit a wider range of microenvironments and resources. Marriage reduces the potential for conflict among families and establishes a basis for cooperation when it comes to fighting with other, unrelated families (1971: 297).

Elman Service has gone so far as to speculate that, in evolutionary terms, cultural rules requiring individuals to marry out of defined groups (i.e., rules of "exogamy") may well have evolved before rules prohibiting marriage within the family (i.e., incest taboos). Writers who stress the integrating function of incest regulation sometimes confuse incest regulation with cultural rules governing or restricting marriage; the two are not the same. Incest regulation pertains to sexual relations and not to marriage per se; if you can marry a particular girl then obviously you can have sexual intercourse with her, but just because one is not prohibited from having sexual relations with a particular girl does not mean that she is a potential spouse. A Brahmin Indian may have sexual relations with a girl of lower caste without being able to marry her; in our own society many people will tolerate sexual relations across racial and/or religious boundaries but will severely criticize and condemn marriage across the same boundaries. It is Service's speculation that incest regulation may have developed in human society to bolster a more fundamental (and prior) need to marry out; rules of incest or no rules of incest, the need for cooperation among groups must have required exogamic regulations: ⊛

> If young females leave the group on marriage, the group is, in a real sense, deprived of them. This must have had some strong emotional consequences. Thus conflict between the emotional desire of individuals to retain their loved ones and the group's rule that they must marry out must have been disruptive. Greater ease, or less poignancy, could be achieved in the loss of the females when their emotional ties within the group were not accompanied by those of sexual relationship. The prohibition of incest, in this speculation, is therefore based on an anticipation of the loss of females. To prohibit sex, of course, does not abolish all emotional ties of parents to children and brother to sister, but certainly the consequences would be much greater if sexual relations had obtained among any of them (1962: 46).

\Unfortunately Service provides no evidence to support his belief that sexual relations invariably produce strong and continuous attachments. ⊘ Would a man necessarily be reluctant to part with a sister with whom he had enjoyed sexual relations if, by so doing, he could be assured of obtaining a new and possibly even more exciting sex mate from another family? In his study of marriage practices among the Rukuba of Nigeria, Jean-Claude Muller found that premarital sexual relations actually involve individuals who *cannot* marry, and that married men may even give their wives in marriage to others (1973: 1563–76)! There is certainly no clear evidence that sexual relations necessarily precludes or interferes with giving the object of sexual attention away in marriage to others.

The Demographic Foundations of Incest Regulation

Some writers have suggested that the demographic attributes of early human populations probably included a short life-span, relatively few offspring surviving to reproductive maturity, wide spacing of childbirths, and a random sex ratio (cf., Slater 1959 and Sussman 1972). Mariam Slater proposed that demographic characteristics such as these may have rendered intrafamilial inbreeding unlikely if not completely impossible. According to Slater,

> early hominids did not mate out because of expediency, sentiment, or an accident that gave them a chance to survive. They did not mate out to form bonds of mutual aid or because of cultural prohibitions. On the contrary, the cooperative bonds as well as the prohibitions must have been consequences of their having already mated out because of structural necessity (1959: 1048–49).

In brief, it is Slater's speculation that it was simply not possible for early human societies to reproduce themselves unless people married out, and that when the demographic formula changed in such a way as to allow for inbreeding, families had already become so involved in cooperative networks and alliances that rules had to be created to keep people marrying out (1959: 1058). While early humans married out for purely demographic reasons, later ones did so for sociological reasons.

It is difficult to evaluate Slater's speculation because we cannot be certain that the fertility and longevity patterns of early hominids resembled those of contemporary hunters and gatherers. Even on the basis of what is known about contemporary hunters and gatherers, moreover, there is no reason to believe that parents always or even usually die or become infertile before their children are old enough to mate with them. As Melvin Ember recently observed,

> a low life expectancy means only that the average life span is, say, 26 years. Such a figure would be generated by the fact that most or many of the total births would die very early, i.e., within the first few years of life, which is still the situation today in many underdeveloped places. For example, if 50 births die at the age of two years (on the average), and there are 50 other births that die at the age of 50 years (on the average), the average life expectancy for these 100 births is the sum (50 x 2) plus (50 x 50) divided by 100, or 26 years. Hence the individuals who survive to reproductive age do not all die by the age of 26. Rather, they may live to a ripe enough old age to permit the possibility of mating with their children (M. Ember n.d.; see also R. Lee 1969).

The Biological Contribution to Incest Regulation

A number of scholars have, at various times, postulated a connection between incest regulation and biological necessity, the idea being that if incest were not prohibited societal continuity would be endangered because people would inbreed and produce defective children—progeny with an impaired capacity for reproduction. In recent years an impressive body of data has emerged to support the belief that consistent close inbreeding will have deleterious genetic consequences, at least in *contemporary* human populations (see Lerner 1958, Morton 1961, Adams and Neil 1967, and Livingstone 1969). But even assuming that incestuous sexual relations have deleterious biological consequences, how and when did humankind come to invent taboos to resolve the problem? It would be a logical error of major proportion to conclude that incest taboos emerged to perform useful social or biological functions unless we are prepared to believe that early humans were aware of the deleterious consequences of consistently close inbreeding since, as David Aberle et al. have noted, such an explanation would be analogous to claiming that noses developed on human faces to hold up eyeglasses (1963: 254).

Evidence from Australia and the Trobriand Islands suggests that not all contemporary peoples may fully appreciate the relationship between copulation and childbirth. The evidence for ignorance has been contested, but when one considers that the interval between copulation and childbirth is long and that the possibility of implantation failure is considerable, it would not be particularly surprising to discover that some people do not grasp the relationship or have an erroneous notion as to its nature. Malinowski claimed that Trobriand Islanders believed that the male function is only to provide a passage of spirits to enter a woman's body, there to assume human form (1929: 153ff., 3, 171). And it has been reported that the people of Rapa in French Polynesia harbor a peculiar notion of the biological mechanisms involved in conception, one that may well account for the fact that they have many more children than they want (Hanson 1970). The Rapans are reportedly convinced that conception requires a coalescence, in the uterus, of blood and semen. Sexual intercourse is avoided during menstruation because it is believed to be contaminating for the male. Couples wishing to avoid conception should also avoid sexual relations during the first few days after menstruation, when a woman is believed to be most fertile. It is during this brief period that fresh blood is said to be entering the uterus. The Rapan believe that the uterus closes to prevent blood seepage after this period and that once closure has taken place conception is impossible.

But whether or not all people recognize it, available evidence indicates that the probability of maladaptive genetic consequences exceeds the probability of adaptive ones where recessive genes are concentrated; the closer the inbreeding, the greater is the concentration of recessive genes. Close inbreeding may have the effect of removing deleterious recessive genes from a gene pool. If a population could afford to lose many children it could conceivably end up with few deleterious genes. But where births are widely spaced, where animals produce few offspring at a time, and where the neonate reaches productive maturity slowly, close inbreeding may so reduce the effective breeding population as to make its survival impossible (Aberle et al 1963: 256–257).

In 1956, a group of scholars met at the Center for Advanced Study in the Behavioral Sciences at Stanford, California, to summarize and consider the accumulated evidence bearing on the origins of incest regulation. The thrust of most research conducted since that time has lent support to the general conclusions arrived at by the participants in that landmark seminar. Aberle summarized their findings in the following way:

> We propose that the adoption of the familial incest taboo was adaptive primarily because of the genetic results of close inbreeding, and that man's familial taboo is to be considered part of the class of devices which limit familial inbreeding among intelligent, slow-maturing animals which bear few offspring at a time and which live in family units. The selection of the taboo, however, we hypothesize, occurred through efforts to solve the problem of sexual competition within the family in a cultural animal with an organized family life. Among the available mechanisms, the incest taboo solved this problem and the genetic problem. Other alternatives solved only one of these problems. Hence it had high selective value. We suggest that it might not have come into being as a response to needs for cooperation between families, but that, once it existed, it did promote this cooperation, which had an adaptive function of little significance for animals. Finally, the familial taboo could be extended, by a simple evalutionary step, to a wider group of kinsmen, with great selective advantage (1963: 264). ☞

Melvin Ember has also expressed the belief that biological factors will ultimately be found to underlie both the origin and extension of incest regulation in human society. He phrased his expectation in terms of a hypothesis regarding first cousin marriage. Ember's formulation of the problem is of special interest because it avoids the trap of attempting to account for one universal phenomenon in terms of another. Although most societies prohibit marriage with all first cousins, there are many that permit marriage with one or more kinds of first cousin. By focusing on cousin marriage, therefore, Ember is attempting to evaluate inbreeding theory by predicting variable extension of the incest taboo to secondary relatives:

> Given . . . that cousin marriage is generally harmful biologically, and assuming that (until perhaps recently) it has been advantageous for most human populations to maximize their reproductive rates, we must ask why there is an unexplainably large minority of societies that permit or even prefer marriage with one or more types of first cousin. Perhaps cousin marriage can be permitted in societies where the chance likelihood of cousin marriage is low (those societies with large genetic isolates). But in societies where cousin marriage is likely to occur frequently by chance (those societies with small genetic isolates), natural selection may favor the prohibition of cousin marriage. (Since the chance likelihood of an individual's marrying a particular type of relative is proportional to the frequency of that type of relative in the genetic isolate, marriage with that type

of relative becomes less likely as the size of the isolate increases.)
(in press).

In testing his prediction cross-culturally, Ember employed indirect meas-
ures of isolate size—the number of levels of political jurisdiction beyond
the community and the average size of communities. His test revealed
that the proportion of societies permitting first cousin marriage increased
with the number of jurisdictional levels, as inbreeding theory would
suggest, and he concluded that,

> consistent with inbreeding theory, the extension of the incest taboo
> to first cousins seems to be most likely in societies with relatively
> small genetic isolates and least likely in societies with relatively
> large isolates. Under certain conditions, exceptions to this rule may
> appear. First, depopulation in middle-sized societies (with popula-
> tions of 1,000 to 25,000) may induce a relaxation of the taboos on
> first cousin marriage (to enlarge the set of eligible mates). Second,
> when the society is very small, marriage with first cousins may be
> permitted in order to provide enough mating possibilities, even if
> depopulation has not occurred (in press).

Despite the evidence that has accumulated in favor of the view that
close inbreeding in contemporary human (and infrahuman) populations
has negative consequences, some writers insist that genetic factors can
account only for the persistence and spread of incest taboos but not for
their initial emergence. Marvin Harris recently observed that,

> as far as a *population* is concerned, inbreeding may produce a higher
> death rate but it may also lead to the gradual elimination of more of
> the deleterious recessive genes than would be the case if completely
> random mating prevailed. In other words, if an inbreeding group is
> able to overcome the higher rate at which homozygotes initially
> appear, it will eventually reach a genetic equilibrium involving a
> lowered percentage of lethal genes. It has often been pointed out
> that the effects of close inbreeding in a small group are largely a
> matter of the original frequency of lethal and deleterious genes
> (1971: 286; cf., Livingstone 1969).

In other words, although close inbreeding may have deleterious consequences with respect to contemporary populations it may not have had
such consequences with respect to paleolithic populations. If the demographic characteristics of early humans allowed for a "weeding out"
process, then early gene pools might have included few lethal recessive
genes and there would have been less danger in inbreeding. Because
contemporary populations do not permit inbreeding, lethal recessive genes
are not as effectively weeded out and, were we suddenly to begin inbreeding, the likelihood of these genes combining would be exacerbated. The

point is that if incest regulations had not been initially imposed, the frequency of potentially deleterious genes would have been lower and inbreeding would not have been maladaptive.

In a similar vein, Melvin Ember suggested the possibility that incest regulations may not have been invented until after humankind had learned to domesticate plants and animals (i.e., some 10,000 years ago). The discovery of domestication made an enormous expansion of population possible and, given a growing breeding population, potentially deleterious recessive genes could accumulate in the gene pool. The reason for this was likelihood that close inbreeding decreased as population expanded. Ember further speculates that neolithic peoples may have *deliberately* adopted the incest taboo and that they may have *purposely* extended it to various close relatives because they *realized* on the basis of actual experience what might happen if they did not do so. He suggests that the difference in reproductive success between consanguineous and non-consanguineous mating could well have been large enough to be noticed during the initial stages of population expansion (when the chance likelihood of close inbreeding was still relatively great).

In conclusion, there can be little doubt that incest regulation functions to prevent the deleterious genetic consequences that would result from consistent, close inbreeding in contemporary populations as well as to regulate intrafamilial relations and promote interfamilial alliances. But the problem of origin has not yet been definitely resolved. It may be, as Aberle et al. have suggested, that nature encouraged the incest taboo because it constituted the only device that could resolve *both* short-term sociological problems and long-term biological ones. According to this speculation the emergence of incest regulation would not have required that people recognize the biological significance of adopting such taboos. But while Aberle and his colleagues have provided a possible explanation for the persistence of incest regulation, they have not satisfactorily accounted for how this particular device was discovered or invented. Even if a few of the world's contemporary peoples do not appreciate the biology of conception, most do and it may well be, as Ember has suggested, that most neolithic peoples also understood the facts of life and deliberately adopted the incest taboo when they became aware that inbreeding was beginning to produce noticeable and adverse biological effects. Once the taboo had been invented it would not be unreasonable to suppose that it would spread quickly and that its sociological rewards would be recognized even by those peoples whose biological sophistication may have left something to be desired.

4

Rules
of
Postmarital Residence

One important correlate of prohibiting sexual relations within the nuclear family is that an individual is obliged to find his or her mate elsewhere. Since husbands and wives are nearly everywhere expected to live together, either the groom, the bride, or both must change residence at marriage. Instances in which neither move, or in which both move to separate residences do occur but are very rare. When we survey the ethnographic record we find that humankind has actually devised a finite number of cultural rules to govern who shall move where when marriage takes place.

Rules of Residence and Their Consequences

"Patrilocal" residence refers to situations in which a bride is normally expected to move to or near the parental home of her groom. Some anthropologists prefer the term "virilocal," which means essentially the same thing except that when this term is employed the stress is on the fact that a woman moves to the location of her husband *wherever* he may be living, even if he is not actually residing with or near his own parents. "Matrilocal" residence refers to situations in which a groom normally moves to or near the parental home of his bride. Here again, some anthropologists, stressing the groom's movement rather than the location of his spouse, prefer the term "uxorilocal." The term "matripatrilocality" is sometimes used to describe situations in which the groom spends a period of residence with his bride's family after marriage, after which the couple shift residence to or near his family. But most anthropologists consider this arrangement a variant of patrilocality. The term "neolocal" is reserved for situations in which a newly married couple normally establishes a domicile separate and apart from either parental home, while "avunculocal" residence describes a pattern in which a couple is expected to live in or near the home of the groom's maternal uncle (i.e., his mother's brother). "Bilocal" refers to a pattern of residence in which a married couple takes up residence with or near *either* parental group. Some anthropologists reserve the term "ambilocal" for a variant of bilocality in which the decision as to which parental group to live with, once made, becomes relatively unalterable. A few consider bilocality no more than a variant of "multilocality," a term intended to embrace all situations in which there are "two or more frequent patterns of consanguineal residence—some combination of matrilocal, patrilocal, and avunculocal" (Ember and Ember 1972: 382). "Duolocality" refers to situations in which a wife and husband continue to live separately after marriage. This is a very rare residence pattern although instances of *de facto* duolocality may not be very well recorded.

While all known and described societies operate primarily in terms of one of the residence rules described above, a comparison of societies reveals that some rules are more commonly adopted than others. Table 4–1 indicates the frequency of various residence rules in the sample of 858 societies coded in the *Ethnographic Atlas* (Murdock 1967). Notice that neolocal societies such as our own are relatively rare as are avunculocal societies. By far the most common postmarital residence pattern is patrilocality. Why is it that in most known and recorded societies it is the woman who is expected to move at marriage, and why should it be that the newly married couple will in most cases settle in or near the parental home of the groom? Phrased in more general terms—what determines the selection of residence rule?

The question as to what factors might predispose a society to adopt one rule of residence or another is important because the particular rule adopted has an impact on other aspects of social organization and provides a point of departure for changes in social organization. It is generally agreed that the rule of postmarital residence is very sensitive to the general economic, technological, social, and cultural conditions under which a people live and that when these circumstances change the rule of residence is likely to reflect such change. Other aspects of social organization are, in turn, sensitive to the prevailing rule of residence and adjust themselves in harmony with it, so that a change in the rule of residence

is likely to generate a series of adaptive modifications throughout the
social structure.

Table 4-1   Prevailing Rules of Residence, by Relative Frequency*

Rule of Residence (With Murdock's Coding)	Number and Percent of All Societies Coded for Residence
Patrilocality	588 (68.5)
Matrilocality	112 (13.1)
Bilocality	73 (8.5)
Neolocality	40 (4.7)
Avunculocality	37 (4.3)
Duolocality	8 (0.9)
Totals	858 (100.0)

* Sample includes all societies coded for residence pattern in the *Ethnographic Atlas* (Murdock 1967).

Two illustrations will indicate the important role of the residence rule.
Consider the impact of residence on family composition and rule of descent. Let us assume that economic conditions favor extension or enlargement of the family. Consistent application of a patrilocal, matrilocal, or avunculocal residence rule will inevitably produce extended families consisting of very different personnel, as figure 4-1 indicates.

It should be clear from this figure that adoption of a patrilocal rule will result in an extended family the core of which consists of males related through males, a matrilocal rule of residence generates an extended family comprising a core of females related through females, while avunculocality produces a family core of males related through females. In short, very different individuals comprise the core members of the extended family in each instance.

If people form groups on the basis of descent from a common ancestor, the way in which descent is traced (e.g., through males only, through females only, or through males for some purposes and through females for others) usually reflects the prevailing rule of postmarital residence. Table 4-2 indicates that most societies in the *Ethnographic Atlas* (Murdock 1967) with a patrilocal residence pattern also have patrilineal kin groups (in 65 percent of all patrilocal cases, or 384 out of 588 cases) although some patrilocal societies employ no unilineal principle of organization. The majority of matrilocal societies (60 percent, or 67 out of 111) lack unilineal descent groups, but where such groups are present they are most likely to be matrilineally organized (in 40 percent of all matrilocal cases, or 44 out of 111 cases). Avunculocality is clearly associated with the presence of matrilineally organized kin groups (97 percent of all avunculocal cases, or 36 out of 37 cases). Societies that have adopted a bilocal or neolocal pattern tend to eschew grouping on the basis of any unilineal

A PATRILOCAL EXTENDED FAMILY

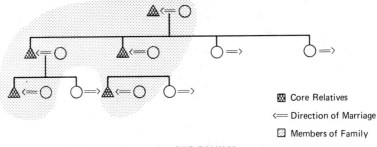

⊠ Core Relatives
⟸ Direction of Marriage
⊡ Members of Family

A MATRILOCAL EXTENDED FAMILY

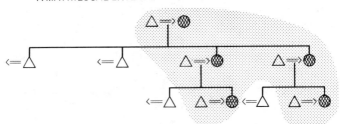

AN AVUNCULOCAL EXTENDED FAMILY

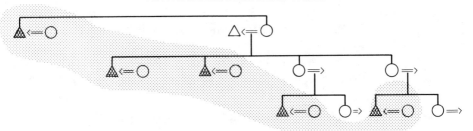

Figure 4-1 A Patrilocal Extended Family

Table 4-2 RULE OF RESIDENCE, BY NATURE OF DESCENT GROUP*

Rule of Residence (With Murdock's Coding)	Patrilineal	Matrilineal	Double Descent	Other
Patrilocal	384	18	25	161
Matrilocal	0	44	0	67
Bilocal	5	14	1	53
Neolocal	6	6	0	28
Avunculocal	0	36	1	0
Duolocal	4	4	0	0

* Sample includes all cases in the *Ethnographic Atlas* (Murdock 1967) coded for both residence and descent.

principle of descent (73 percent of the bilocal cases and 70 percent of the neolocal societies lack unilineal descent). If we consider only those societies that have for one reason or another formed extrafamilial kin groups, we find that those with patrilineal descent group are overwhelmingly patrilocal (96 percent of all patrilineal cases, or 384 out of 399 societies), most matrilineal societies are either matrilocal or avunculocal (66 percent of all matrilineal cases, or 80 out of 122 societies), and societies that employ both unilineal principles simultaneously (i.e., those with double descent) are most commonly patrilocal (in 93 percent of all double descent cases, or 25 out of 27 instances). While most of the societies that do not group people in terms of either a unilineal or double unilineal principle of descent are patrilocal (52 percent of all "other"), a number are either matrilocal (22 percent) or bilocal (17 percent of "other"). [In summary, while there is no invariable relationship or association between the prevailing rule of residence and the nature of extrafamilial kin groups in society, there does tend to be a harmony or agreement between the two phenomena. Adoption of a prevailing unilocal rule of residence (e.g., patrilocality, matrilocality, or avunculocality) does seem to affect the way in which descent groups are organized. ๏

Although the prevailing rule of postmarital residence, extended family organization, and the principle of descent are commonly consistent, perfect harmony is clearly lacking. George P. Murdock some years ago suggested (1949: 137–38, 197–98) that incongruities may result from what he termed "time lag"—from the fact that a recent change in pattern of residence has not yet made itself felt in other aspects of social organization. Inconsistencies of this sort may therefore signal systems in the process of change.

On the Determinants of Residence

Let us accept that rule of residence influences other aspects of social organization and return to the basic question of determination. What accounts for the different frequencies of various residence patterns and preferences in human society? What factors might predispose a people to adopt one practice or another? We have already suggested, in passing, that changes in fundamental life conditions can exert pressures to modify an existing residence pattern. This general notion led Murdock to observe that,

so diverse are the casual factors in social change, and so few are the alternatives in residence rules, that nearly any society, whatever its level of culture and existing forms of social organization, can probably encounter particular concatenations of circumstances that will favor the development of any one of the alternative rules of residence (1949: 203).

In other words, since the number of residence patterns actually employed is limited, and since all of them are found at all levels of cultural complexity, no statements of an evolutionary nature can be made about them. Similar causal factors may be found at any level of cultural complexity. However, a consideration of the factors that might incline a society to adopt one rule of residence rather than another, reveals reasons for questioning Murdock's conclusions.

Although we noted earlier that incest taboos everywhere require that some members of the family marry out, we left aside the question as to *which* members of the family should leave. Cross-cultural comparisons indicate that, in most societies, it is the female rather than the male who moves at marriage, and some writers have even suggested that patrilocality probably preceded all other rules of residence in man's developmental history. Elman Service speculated, for example, that paleolithic hunters and gatherers were most likely to have been predominantly patrilocal (1962: 65).[1] "Composite" bands, which lack a consistent unilocal pattern of residence, are likely the result of recent disruption—of depopulation and consequent group reconstruction.

C. R. Ember recently completed a cross-cultural study that has a direct bearing on Service's speculation (in press); she discovered that, among a sample of contemporary hunters and gatherers, depopulation does in fact predict residential flexibility ("multilocality"). She also discovered that flexibility in terms of postmarital residence is more likely in hunting-gathering societies which have fewer than fifty persons in the local group for more than half the year than in those with larger groups. The explanation offered is that small groups are probably more subject to chance fluctuations in the ratio of males to females at birth and, for this reason, may have greater difficulty maintaining a unilocal rule of residence. In short, Ember's evidence supports the hypothesis that multilocality is likely to be practiced among hunters and gatherers that have experienced depopulation or which live in local groups averaging fifty persons or less for most of the year. Of what relevance are these findings to Service's speculation that paleolithic hunting-gathering peoples were probably patrilocal? As was indicated in an earlier chapter, hunting-gathering populations once lived in areas of the world much less marginal than those in which we now find them. It is quite possible that, prior to contact and consequent depopulation, their bands may have been larger than fifty for most of the year and that multilocality

[1] For an opposing point of view see Martin 1969. On the basis of data on hunter-gatherers in South America, Martin suggests that early hunter-gatherers may have more commonly been matrilocal.

may also have been far less common among such peoples than is the case today. We cannot be certain which unilocal mode of residence was most common in paleolithic society, but we should note that patrilocality is most common among contemporary unilocal hunter-gatherers.

Table 4-3   RELATIONSHIP BETWEEN RULE OF RESIDENCE AND
MEAN SIZE OF LOCAL COMMUNITIES*

Rule of Residence	Mean Size of Local Communities		
	Fewer than 99 Persons	100 to 5,000 but in Absence of Indigenous Urban Aggregations	One or More Indigenous Urban Aggregations of More than 5,000
Patrilocal	111 *societies*	135	59
Matrilocal	32	33	3
Bilocal	24	16	3
Neolocal	5	11	10
Avunculocal	7	9	1
Duolocal	0	2	1

* Sample includes all societies in the *Ethnographic Atlas* (Murdock 1967) coded for both prevailing rule of residence and mean community size.

Table 4-3 indicates that a unilocal rule of residence is far more common than either bilocality or neolocality regardless of mean community size (one possible indicator of cultural complexity), and that patrilocality is the most common pattern at all levels. While all rules of residence occur at all levels of complexity measured in these terms, we find that some rules are significantly more common at one level than at another. When we say that one phenomenon (like frequency of a particular rule of residence) is "significantly" associated with another (like mean community size), we mean that the observed statistical association would be very unlikely to occur accidentally or simply by chance. In this sense neolocality is significantly more likely to be found in societies with a mean community size over five thousand than in societies with a mean community size under five thousand. Bilocality, on the other hand, is significantly more likely in societies with a mean community size under ninety-nine than over ninety-nine; and of the unilocal residence rules, patrilocality is significantly more likely in societies with a mean community size greater than five thousand than in societies with a mean size of community under five thousand. But while some rules of residence do occur more frequently at certain levels of societal complexity than at others, we cannot predict the adoption of the different rules simply in terms of level of complexity. How then might we go about specifying the conditions that would encourage adoption of one residence practice over another?

A number of speculations have been proposed to account for the apparent propensity of humankind for patrilocality. Some writers have suggested that patrilocality is somehow more "natural" inasmuch as males are, by nature, dominant. But the ethnographic record indicates that males maintain social and political dominance in all human societies—in matrilocal as well as in patrilocal settings. Others have proposed a linkage between rule of residence and economic function: brothers are more often kept together because their contribution to group subsistence is more important. This is said to be especially true in hunting-gathering societies since men are, after all, the hunters. There are a number of problems with such explanations simply on logical grounds. Even in hunting-gathering bands that depend heavily on women's work for the bulk of caloric consumption the rule of residence is normally patrilocal. Although the Yahgan of Tierra del Fuego subsist mainly on shellfish gathered by women, they have adopted a patrilocal rule of residence. Another difficulty with an explanation in terms of economic contribution has to do with how we are to measure such contribution—shall we consider caloric input, time spent in productive tasks, protein contribution, provision of biologically necessary trace elements, or perhaps contribution to group defense? Where protein sources (e.g., animals and fish) are few or where they fluctuate in availability, the economic importance of male activities (i.e., of the hunters) may be greater than that of women despite the fact that they spend less time and/or energy at their work than do the women and even though their caloric contribution is less.

Elman Service has noted that hunting and defense, almost invariably male occupations, require a greater degree of cooperation than the kinds of occupations normally engaged in by women, and he suggested that it may be the greater degree of cooperation characteristic of male occupations that predisposes a society to keep brothers rather than sisters together. According to Service,

> competition among societies could have been the most important cause of virilocality, for if offense-defense requirements are important, then the trusting cooperation among brothers and other closely linked male relatives would be more important than anything else (1962: 49).

One could argue that even where fighting is infrequent, the possibility of violence would place a premium on practices and customs which serve to maximize fighting efficiency. On the other hand there is no hard evidence which could support the belief that men brought up together necessarily fight better than those that have not been brought up together. Our own military forces are certainly not predicated on such an assumption. Perhaps, at the most primitive fighting levels, it is preferable to keep known quantities at home rather than to accept unknown quantities—but the question remains open (cf., Kloos 1963).

Melvin and C. R. Ember recently (1971) employed a worldwide sample of societies to empirically evaluate the hypothesis that the sex which contributes most to subsistence is the sex most likely to be aggregated after marriage. They found no statistically significant association between contribution to subsistence by sex and rule of residence in the direction predicted. The Embers also tested a version of Service's notion that rule of residence is somehow related to cooperation, especially in fighting, but found no greater prevalence of patrilocality among societies that fight more often. They then hypothesized that if fighting ever occurs *within* a society ("internal warfare"), such a society is most likely to be patrilocal, whereas if fighting is always *between* societies ("external"), then a society is likely to be matrilocal if men are so occupied fighting that women have to undertake most of the subsistence work. Their hypothesis can be outlined as follows:

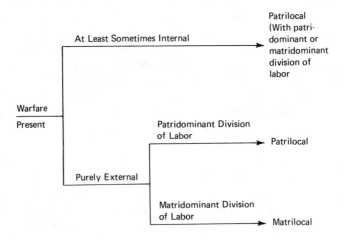

Figure 4-2   Warfare, Division of Labor, and Rule of Residence

Underlying this hypothesis is the assumption that men normally do more subsistence work than women unless the nature of warfare prevents them from doing so; that all things being equal, the division of labor is more likely to be patridominant simply because women everywhere must divert some of their energies and time to childbearing and child care.

The Ember hypothesis is particularly interesting because it combines elements of both the economic and defense-offense interpretations discussed earlier. When they tested their formulation in terms of a sample of societies drawn from the *Human Relations Area Files* the Embers found that it had statistical support. In other words, their hypothesis did predict, with a high degree of success, whether a people would be patrilocal or matrilocal in terms of the nature of warfare and the division of labor.

Although the proposed association between internal warfare and patrilocality enjoys statistical support it nevertheless requires some further explanation. Why should a society tend to be patrilocal if fighting is internal regardless of which sex contributes most to subsistence? To answer this question we will have to make a brief diversion. A few years ago, David Schneider (1961: vii–29), pointed to a fundamental difference between societies in which descent is traced to a common ancestor exclusively through males as opposed to those in which descent is traced exclusively through females—that is, between "patrilineal" and "matrilineal" societies. The difference has to do with how descent group membership is determined and who provides authority. In patrilineal societies a child is placed in the descent group of his father and his father exercises authority over him or her (i.e., group placement and authority are both vested in males). While authority in matrilineal societies is similarly vested in males, children are placed in the descent groups of their mothers (see figure 4-3). Because men continue to exercise authority over their sisters' children in matrilineal societies males cannot be completely released to wander off at marriage. In a patrilineal context, on the other hand, there is no reason why a woman cannot marry a man who lives far from her brother's home since she performs no vital functions in terms of either determining descent group membership or in exercising authority vis-à-vis her brother or his children. We noted earlier that matrilineal societies are most commonly also matrilocal and, as Murdock suggested, if a people are matrilocal they are less likely to marry out of their home communities or far from them than if they are patrilocal (1949: 213–14).

Peter Kloos (1963) has provided additional cross-cultural support for the view that the tendency of matrilocal-matrilineal societies to be community endogamous is closely related to the nature of authority and leadership. He found that if succession to authority in matrilocal societies is

Rule of Descent

		Patrilineal	Matrilineal
Sociological Function	Authority	Male	Male
	Group Placement	Male	Female

Figure 4-3   Sociological Function, Sex, and Rule of Descent

determined by descent (i.e., is matrilineally ascribed) rather than being achieved without regard to descent, then at least *some* males will marry endogamously and communities will tend to be endogamous. This particular difference between matrilineal-matrilocal societies and patrilineal-patrilocal societies is relevant to the nature of warfare. As the Embers point out, if people are fighting internally (i.e., between neighboring communities), then we should be able to predict that they are *not* matrilocal since a man might otherwise find himself initiating hostilities in his sister's community against the very community in which he or his brothers are living (Ember & Ember 1971: 582).

As it turns out, where fighting is internal people *are* most likely to be patrilocal, even if the preceding explanation for the association is incorrect (cf., Van Velzen et al. 1960 and Otterbein 1965). Where fighting is purely external, on the other hand, the rule of residence can be either patrilocal or matrilocal depending on whether or not the nature of fighting diverts men from subsistence activities.

But an important question remains unanswered—does the rule of residence determine the nature of fighting or vice-versa? Are we to understand that people do not fight internally because they are matrilocal (i.e., because fighting locally would mean pitting sons-in-law who have come to live in one's community against sons who have left to live in neighboring communities), or rather, does the nature of warfare determine the rule of residence? The Embers clearly prefer the latter solution and explain their choice on the grounds that "if fighting occurs between neighboring communities, families would want to keep their fighters at home for protection" (1971: 584). In this view, then, matrilocal residence is avoided because people are fighting internally.

In a more recent paper, W. T. Divale (1974) also focused upon the relationship between type of warfare and rule of residence but suggested a different causal sequence. In brief, he proposed that recent migration (i.e., during the past five hundred years) into an inhabited area stimulates matrilocality, a pattern of residence which is adaptive because it produces internal harmony and purely external warfare. Matrilocality is presumed by Divale to encourage internal harmony by scattering consanguineously related males and avoiding fraternal factionalism.

The Embers had proposed that warfare affects residence, whereas, Divale's theory suggested the opposite. Observing that, since only half the migrating societies in Divale's sample are matrilocal, migration can at best be considered only a partial cause of matrilocal residence (1974: 137), C. R. Ember has nonetheless admitted that Divale's findings were impressive enough to require modification of the earlier model proposed by herself and her husband:

The new model still assumes that matrilocality will arise in those societies in which women contribute a great deal to subsistence and which have a purely external pattern of warfare; and that patrilocality will be found whenever internal warfare is present or when men contribute more to subsistence, even if warfare is purely external. The change in the model comes from a consideration of the conditions under which warfare is expected to be internal or purely external. I suggest that, under warfare-provoking conditions, small societies will generally fight purely externally. Exceptions would be expected where there is severe physical or social circumscription . . . but purely external warfare may be expected among small societies which have accessible neighbors and which are generally able to beat those neighbors. In contrast, societies which are small and isolated, small and not generally successful in intersocietal fighting, or large in population or territory may all be expected to develop some internal warfare under warfare-provoking conditions (1974: 145–46).

Ember reasons that if we assume that purely external warfare is a function of small population size (i.e., societies less than or equal to twenty-one thousand in population) and of consistent success in intersocietal fighting, then the pool of small, relatively successful societies should be larger among migratory societies because, as Divale's data indicate, migratory societies have a higher proportion of small societies and because those intrusive societies which survived to be recorded must have been consistently successful in warfare. Intersocietal competition has probably also been especially severe in the case of migrating societies (1974: 146–47). According to Ember, then, it is because the pool of small *and* successful societies is much larger among migrating societies than among nonmigrating societies that the possibility of matrilocality is greater among them (1974: 147).

We have thus far only been discussing factors that might select for a prevailing patrilocal or matrilocal residence pattern. But under what circumstances would a people be likely to eschew a matrilocal or patrilocal rule of residence in favor of some other residential possibility? Some scholars have suggested a connection between bilocality and migration. G. P. Murdock proposed, for example, that:

on a relatively low level of culture, the adoption of a migratory life in unstable bands seems particularly conducive to this rule of residence. A family may pitch its tent or erect its hut near the father's relatives at one compsite and near the mother's at the next, or if they belong to different bands it may reside with either or shift from one to the other (1949: 204).

Underlying Murdock's suggestion is the implicit assumption that conditions favor collective rather than individual economic activities otherwise neolocality would probably be more likely than bilocality.

Another factor that has been suggested as an inducement to bilocality is sexual equality. A man might be inclined to live with his wife's family if her status or inheritance prospects were superior to his own (e.g., Murdock 1949: 204). Still others have proposed that fluctuating economic resources may play some role in encouraging a preference for bilocality. Adoption of a bilocal residence pattern would enable a people to compensate for temporary local shortages (e.g., Eggan 1966: 58–64). And we earlier drew attention to Service's speculation that most instances of bilocality among primitive peoples might be accounted for in terms of depopulation. The logic, simply put, is that the severe depopulation which followed contact with Europeans may have forced many primitive peoples to reconstitute their local groups in such a way as to maintain groups of optimal demographic and economic size. This speculation assumes, of course, that in most primitive and noncommercial settings families are obliged to work cooperatively so depopulation would reduce the economic feasibility of maintaining a strict unilocal pattern of postmarital residence. A recent attempt to evaluate the relative merits of these various explanations (Ember and Ember 1972) indicated that depopulation constituted the best predictor of multilocality in noncommercial settings; only this factor accounted for *most* cases of multilocality in such societies. We might observe, in passing, that this finding is consistent with Service's speculation that hunters and gatherers may have been more commonly patrilocal than bilocal in precontact times.

What conditions might favor a preference for neolocal residence? A number of years ago Murdock (1949: 203) suggested that any condition which isolates or emphasizes either the individual or the nuclear family (i.e., a family consisting of husband, wife, and their children if any) should also favor a propensity for neolocal residence. Scarce resources would certainly have this effect (and might account for neolocality among such peoples as the Eskimo), and by encouraging social and physical mobility, industry and commerce may also stimulate a stress upon both the nuclear family and neolocal residence. In fact some scholars have even suggested that the trend to nuclear families and neolocality so widespread today is actually a relatively recent one which results from the development of industry and commerce in human society. Ralph Linton once suggested that "the greater the opportunities for individual economic profit provided by any social-cultural situation the weaker the ties of extended kinship will become" (1952: 84), and Julian Steward (1959) proposed that the emergence of a cash economy is what leads to individualization of land tenure and hence to a weakening of kin ties. Nuclear families become economically independent and residence becomes neolocal as the rise of commercial exchange makes it possible for individuals to sell their labor and the products of their labor to buy what they need to live. Several years ago M. Ember (1967) tested cross-culturally the hypothesis that the presence of some commercial exchange in society will be associated with some, even if only alternative, neolocality. Statistical support for the hypothesis was obtained. Although commercialization may in fact stimulate a propensity for neolocality I am inclined to agree with Goode (1963) that the relationship between commercialization, industrialization, and the nature of kinship organization is still poorly understood. This will be further explored in chapter 7 in an examination of the family.

Avunculocality is characteristic of very few societies and little is known about the factors likely to encourage this pattern of residence. Some years ago G. P. Murdock suggested that patrilocality and avunculocality may constitute alternative responses to similar causes (1949: 211). In brief, assuming that conditions in a matrilocal setting change in such a way as to encourage keeping men rather than women together, then a society is likely to shift to avunculocality rather than to patrilocality if matrilineal descent constitutes an important organizational principle and if there are no reasons why a man cannot go to live with his mother's brother (see also Eyde and Postal 1961). There may be a connection between a preference for the avunculocal pattern and the presence of strong matrilineal descent groups (since this rule of residence responds to the need for aggregating related males without violating or disrupting a prevailing principle of matrilineal descent), but Murdock's requirement that avunculocality must be feasible actually confuses matters since he fails to indicate the conditions that might preclude avunculocality.

In a recent study (1974a) M. Ember obtained some empirical support for the hypothesis that there will be no switch to avunculocality unless a previously matrilocal society also has matrilineal descent groups. A cross-cultural sample of societies revealed that all avunculocal societies have matrilineal descent groups, in contrast to matrilocal societies which do not all have them, and also in contrast to patrilocal societies which do not all have patrilineal descent groups. But why do avunculocal societies have to retain unilineal descent groups and why must they be matrilineal? On the basis of an earlier study (Ember, Ember and Pasternak, 1974), Ember notes that descent groups are likely to be retained where warfare is present, and he further proposes that they are especially likely to be matrilineal in societies which recently began to fight internally if there has been a high male mortality rate. In short, internal fighting encourages descent group maintenance but, given an abnormally high male mortality, such groups can be easily maintained only by retaining the principle of descent through females. Matrilocal societies thus become avunculocal rather than patrilocal to retain matrilineality in the face of an abnormally high male mortality rate. Although Ember has cross-cultural evidence consistent with his theory, this kind of evidence, being synchronic in nature, can only support the associations proposed: it can neither confirm nor allow us to reject the causal sequence suggested, as Ember himself points out. The evidence confirms an association between avunculocality, matrilineality, high male-mortality, and internal warfare, but it does not indicate which variables are causes and which are effects. Only ethnohistorical analyses of particular cases can ultimately tell us that.

Less is known about duolocality than about avunculocality. Since the recorded instances of this residential preference are so few (see for example, Gough 1964, Befu 1968, Muller 1973, and Watson 1974), it is impossible to generalize about them in any convincing or controlled fashion. Harumi Befu (1968) described one instance of duolocal residence found in central Japan where, until about seventy-five years ago, there existed a cluster of hamlets (Nakagiri) in which husbands and wives lived separately for life. They remained in their respective natal households, which were composed of as many as twenty or thirty individuals. Only the household head brought his wife into the household. Befu attempted to account for both the size of these households and the duolocal pattern of residence in ecological and economic terms. Because people in Nakagiri were living near starvation levels there was, according to Befu, an unusual pressure to reduce per capita expenses by avoiding family partition. The nature of agriculture in Nakagiri reportedly also favored the formation and persistence of large households capable of providing large labor forces. Befu suggests that extended families consisting of several married siblings are highly volatile and fragile. So long as family partition is possible the competitive stresses that eventually emerge between the married couples that comprise such families need not be suppressed. However, where partition is difficult or highly disadvantageous, any stimulus to family division will be highly maladaptive. This was especially the case in Nakagiri:

> When branching became less and less feasible in Nakagiri, probably about the late eighteenth and early nineteenth centuries, it became disruptive to the maintenance of the household—for reasons already stated—to bring in affines and permanently retain collateral couples. As a result, male members of the household were discouraged from bringing their wives in, and men were forced to delay this second state of their marriage. After branching became a virtual impossibility, coresidence of spouses ceased (1968: 317).

Although we still have much to learn about the factors that incline a people to adopt one rule of residence or another we have already made considerable headway with respect to this important question. Still greater strides will be taken in the future on the basis of what we have already accomplished, as the quantity of our data sources increases and as new and more sophisticated hypotheses are formulated and subjected to empirical test.

5

Forms
of Marriage

Incest regulations, however, and for whatever reasons they emerged, inevitably required people to find mates outside their own nuclear or conjugal families, and marriage is the institution by means of which this is accomplished. Let us therefore turn our attention to "marriage" and consider first the range of phenomena commonly referred to when this term is employed. Let us also determine the extent to which all societies can be said to have marriage. Finally we must investigate the forms marriage takes in human societies and attempt to account for the variations observed.

The Meaning of Marriage

Most definitions of "marriage" require that the spouses live together, that their union be ritually recognized in some fashion, or that their relationship be one that clearly defines sexual rights. The difficulty with such criteria is that, individually or in combination, they do not enable us to include all ethnographic situations that we intuitively feel ought to be embraced in a general discussion of marriage. This is one reason for the fact that a number of anthropologists have struggled to formulate a definition of marriage that would truly apply cross-culturally. Let us consider a few of the definitions that have been proposed.

G. P. Murdock has suggested that marriage exists "only when the economic and the sexual [functions] are united into one relationship" (1949: 8). He believes that this combination of functions occurs *only* in marriage and that marriage, thus defined, is a characteristic of every human society. In all societies, said Murdock, marriage "involves residential cohabitation, and in all of them it forms the basis of the nuclear family" (1949: 8). There are a number of difficulties inherent in Murdock's definition of marriage; for one thing there are ethnographic instances in which husbands and wives do not live together. In a number of developing and industrial contexts, for example, husbands commonly leave home and hearth to find employment or seek their fortunes elsewhere (e.g., Watson 1974; cf., Gough 1968, Befu 1968, and Muller 1973). To require that a married couple engage in sexual and economic cooperation is also less than satisfactory. Consider the Nayar, a people of India's Malabar Coast. A Nayar woman actually enjoyed several mates. She lived with none of them and did not cooperate with any of them in an economic sense. "Husbands" visited their "wives" after dinner and left before breakfast; they contributed nothing of material significance to the subsistence of their "wives" or "children," but were responsible instead for the well-being of their sisters and of their sisters' children (Gough 1968). In our own society it is not uncommon for a couple to share a common household and budget for varying periods without the benefit of a legal or ritual marriage.

A somewhat different definition of marriage was proposed in a volume entitled, *Notes and Queries* (Seligman 1951):

> Marriage is a union between a man and a woman such that children born to the woman are the recognized legitimate offspring of both parents (1951: 110).

But what then are we to make of the Nuer, a people of the Upper Nile, who have a minor form of marriage involving not a man and a woman but a woman and another woman? Elman Service recently described this unusual arrangement as follows:

> There is also a kind of marriage between two women, one of which, the "husband," is usually barren. Children are begotten to the couple by the service of a male kinsman or friend. The "husband" administers the family just as would a man and is the "father" of the children (1971: 151).

The Nuer are not the only people who make allowances for marriage between individuals of the same sex. Among the Cheyenne, Indians of the Great Plains, marriage sometimes joined men (Hoebel 1960: 77), and

E. E. Evans-Pritchard (1970) has reported a form of marriage based on sexual inversion, or homosexuality, among the Azande of the Sudan:

> It was the custom for members of bachelor companies, some of whom would always be living in barracks at court, to take boy-wives. This was undoubtedly brought about by the scarcity of marriageable women in the days when the nobility and also the richer commoners kept large harems and were able to acquire it more easily than poorer men. Most young men consequently married late—well into their twenties and thirties—and, because girls were engaged (in a legal sense married) very young, often at birth, the only way youths could obtain satisfaction from a woman was in adultery. But that was a very dangerous solution (1970: 1429).

Evans-Pritchard indicates that he employs the terms "wife," "husband," and "marriage," in connection with this relationship intentionally because, so long as it lasted, it constituted "a legal union on the model of a normal marriage" (1970: 1429). The "husband" was expected to pay the boy's parents a bride-price and if someone else had sexual relations with the boy-wife he could be sued for adultery. The couple addressed each other as "husband" and "wife" and the latter was expected to perform a variety of services appropriate to an ordinary wife (1970: 1429–30). Marriages between individuals of like sex are certainly not unknown even in our own society: the following excerpt was taken from the *New York Post*, April 16, 1971:

> A number of "married" homosexuals filed joint income tax returns last year and got away with it. They planned to do the same this year. . . . On the legality of a "married" homosexual couple filing a joint return, the IRS has no policy. "It comes down to the point where we recognize a marriage if that marriage is recognized under state law," the spokesman said.

And what are we to do with the Kwakiutl, Indians of the northwest coast of this continent? It was customary, among these people, for chiefly prerogatives to pass from a titled man to his grandson through a son-in-law. Special marriage ceremonies were reserved for situations in which a chief found himself daughterless. A man who wanted to acquire use of a chiefly crest or privilege could marry the title-holder's son; if there was no son, then a prospective "son-in-law" could marry a part of the title-holder's body! Should we include such practices in a general discussion of marriage?

Many people permit and recognize marriage with a ghost under certain circumstances. A Nuer man may marry a woman on behalf of his deceased brother, who will be considered the "father" of her children (Service 1971: 151). Marriage with a ghost has also been reported among the Chinese (see, for example, Topley 1955 and 1956; Friedman 1970: 165–66; and Smith 1970: 227). In traditional China, where marriage was considered more important as a device for perpetuating and linking families than for joining particular individuals, such marriage served several purposes. Important alliances were sometimes arranged between families through the betrothal or engagement of infants. If one of the prospective spouses did not manage to survive to adulthood, this did not necessarily mean that a potentially profitable "affinal" relationship (i.e., a relationship through marriage) would have to be abandoned; the marriage could still be consummated with the ghost of the deceased party. A dead groom's family could still enjoy the benefits and labor of a daughter-in-law. If the groom survived the bride, on the other hand, he had the option of taking a second (living) wife. Do arrangements between the living and dead also belong in a general definition and discussion of marriage?

If marriage occurs at all among the Nayar (Gough 1968), it involves a woman and several men. The legitimacy of children requires at least two fathers of appropriate caste—a ritual father and one or more admitted biological fathers. Unless a woman is ritually married to a man of appropriate caste, and unless her child's paternity is vouched for by one or more visiting husbands of appropriate caste (not necessarily by the actual progenitor), a child cannot enter the caste or descent group of his or her mother and therefore becomes a social pariah. This situation prompted E. K. Gough to suggest yet another definition of marriage:

> Marriage is a relationship established between a woman and one or more other persons, which provides that a child born to the woman under circumstances not prohibited by the rules of the relationship, is accorded full birth-status rights common to normal members of his society or social stratum (1968: 68).

Enough has been said to indicate how difficult it is to arrive at a definition of marriage that will satisfy all situations and be acceptable to all anthropologists and social scientists. It is unlikely that the matter has been resolved with Gough's definition (cf., Harris 1971: 273–75). My own feeling is that we should avoid becoming obsessed with the task of formulating a definition without exceptions or objections. It is not really so vital that we establish that all people have marriage. It is far more important that we adopt a clear and explicit working definition that will embrace most ethnographic cases and that we concentrate our energies rather on relating "marriage" so defined to other cultural phenomena. Gough's definition would serve us quite well in this regard.

Polygamous Marriage

However one chooses to define it, the ethnographic record reveals that marriage takes a limited number of forms. In our own society the preferred and only tolerated mode of marriage is "monogamous"—we allow an individual to have only one spouse at a time. But societies that allow only monogamous marriage are relatively rare; some 83 percent of the societies listed in the *Ethnographic Atlas* (Murdock 1967) permit some form of "polygamy," or marriage with more than one spouse at the same time (see Table 5-1). Polygamous marriage, in turn, may take one or two forms—in a "polygynous" marriage a man has more than one spouse simultaneously, in a "polyandrous" marriage a woman has more than one husband at the same time. The number of societies that allow polyandrous marriage are actually very few; about 83 percent of all the societies coded for marriage in the *Atlas* allow polygynous marriage as against less than 1 percent that allow polyandrous marriage. Another very rare form of marriage is "group" marriage, in which several men are married to a group of women with no dyadic pairing such that one particular man is considered married to one particular woman. This form of marriage is neither common nor customary in any known human society.

Table 5-1   SOCIETIES IN THE ETHNOGRAPHIC ATLAS
(Murdock, 1967) BY TYPE OF MARRIAGE ALLOWED

Type of Marriage	Number of Cases	Percent All Coded Cases
Monogamous Only	137	16
Polygynous At Least Occasionally	712	83
Polyandrous Allowed	4	0
Unknown (No Data Coded)	9	1
Totals	862	100

A word of caution is appropriate at this point. We should recall that what a people "prefer" or "believe" they do many not precisely correspond to what they actually do. Some anthropologists classify a society as polygynous if such marriage is "preferred," or if it is "said to be" common. But ethnographic descriptions do not always clearly indicate the extent to which behavior conforms to either cultural ideals or expressed beliefs, although a difference between belief and practice is important in its own right and demands investigation. If we are to compare societies, therefore, it would be well to compare them in the same terms—that is in terms of preferences, beliefs, or actual behavior. Since the difference between informant impressions as regards the relative frequencies of different marriage modes and the actual frequencies of such modes are usually not very great we will not go far astray if we assume, for purposes of cross-cultural comparison, that forms said to be common probably are.

We must also keep in mind that the rules which govern second or subsequent marriages sometimes differ from those that regulate first marriages, and that adherence to ideas may differ dramatically in the case of first and subsequent marriages. In some societies, for example, it is said that a man should marry the sister of his deceased wife (sororate marriage) or that a woman should marry the brother of her dead husband (levirate marriage). In some polygynous societies it is claimed that the sister of one's wife makes an ideal second wife (sororal polygyny), and in some polyandrous settings the husband's brother makes an especially suitable second husband (fraternal polyandry). It is also possible for different models of preferential marriage to apply to different children. Jean-Claude Muller has reported that such is the case among the Rukuba of Nigeria, for example, where marriage preferences depend on birth order (1973: 1569). But the fact that people express a preference for one or more customs regarding choice of spouse does not necessarily mean that they commonly or frequently behave in conformance with expressed preference.

Polygynous Marriage

Under what conditions might a preference for polygynous marriage be expected? Some scholars have suggested that the relative popularity of this rule in human societies is the result of a species predisposition for plural spouses (e.g., Linton 1968: 285). But if men are born with such a "natural" propensity do women come equipped with an opposite one which encourages them to share a common husband? If polygyny reflects a basic and innate species predisposition, furthermore, why is this marital preference not characteristic of all human societies? A connection has been suggested between the popularity of polygyny and certain supposedly universal human biological characteristics—male dominance and the constant sexual urges and appetites of the human animal. Ralph Linton, who took this position, suggested that these innate attributes would stimulate an inclination to polygyny especially in a situation in which females outnumber males. There are in fact more females than males in many primitive societies, probably because men engage in more dangerous occupations and because of higher infant mortality rates among

males (Linton 1968: 281–86). One anthropologist (Osmond 1965) has presented evidence which suggests that polygyny is favored by societies
with simpler socioeconomic structures while monogamy is favored by
those with more complex structures, and another scholar (Ember 1974b)
has recently obtained empirical evidence for a connection between high
male mortality and polygyny in a sample of societies lacking commercial
exchange (and hence an opportunity for single women to make their
livings independently). Melvin Ember found that polygynous societies
were significantly more likely to have an unbalanced sex-ratio in favor
of females than those which were nonpolygynous.

Another explanation that has been proposed links the preference for
polygyny to the adoption of a long postpartum sex taboo—that is, to the
custom of prohibiting a resumption of sexual intercourse between spouses
for a year or more after birth of a child. John Whiting, who first suggested this association (1969), reasoned as follows: Societies low in sources
of protein are especially subject to an often fatal disease of childhood
known as kwashiorkor and customs that might serve to mitigate protein
deficiency ought to be encouraged in such contexts. In protein deficient
settings breast-feeding may provide the major source of protein for infants.
Since a long postpartum sex taboo would reduce the likelihood of closely
spaced successive pregnancies, the effect of which would be to reduce the
protein available per child from this source during critical stages of their
growth, we should expect this taboo to be especially common in protein
deficient areas. And where we find a long postpartum sex taboo we might
also expect to discover frequent resort to polygynous marriage as a means
of alleviating long periods of sexual deprivation. Whiting obtained some
cross-cultural support for his hypothesis; it turned out that societies
dependent on root and tree crops (presumably low protein societies) are
more likely than others to have a long postpartum sex taboo, and there
did seem to be a statistical association between the presence of this taboo
and a preference for polygyny. There are some logical difficulties with
Whiting's explanation for the observed associations, however. Why, for
example, should a man denied access to his wife for a year or more necessarily have to "marry" another woman to satisfy his sexual needs? The
problem could be alleviated by extra-marital alliances, masturbation, or
perhaps even by resorting to cold swims in nearby rivers.

Polyandrous Marriage

The *Ethnographic Atlas* (Murdock 1967) lists only four societies which
allow polyandrous marriage: the Tibetans, Sherpa, Toda, and Marquesans.
This form of marriage is clearly uncommon and some people have sug-

gested that it will appear only in situations of extreme economic deprivation, where one man alone cannot possibly support a wife and children.
Others have suggested that polyandry is likely to be found in association
with female infanticide—the practice of killing some female infants at
birth. Still others propose that extreme poverty might well be the catalyst
for both cultural practices—for polyandry and for female infanticide (e.g.,
Linton 1968: 285). At present very little is known about the conditions
that encourage polyandry mainly because it is so rare a phenomenon. It
might be useful and suggestive to consider one relatively well described
case.

Reports on marriage practices in Tibet have been very contradictory;
some writers claim that the Tibetans are monogamous, others that they
are polygynous, and still others that they practice polyandry. In one
recent study (Goldstein 1971), evidence was presented which suggests
that the answer to this apparent puzzle may depend on which economic
stratum of the Tibetan population we consider.

Tibetans reportedly believe that households containing two or more
married siblings are highly unstable; the wives soon get to fighting and a
family partition is soon precipitated. Because Tibetan custom allowed
brothers to share equally in a family estate at the time of family division,
it was essential for families of certain economic status to make a special
effort to avoid partition if at all possible, and it was in families of this
particular sort that polyandry, while not considered desirable, was tolerated and commonplace. In short, polyandry enabled a family to avoid
a major cause of family division—quarreling between wives. Family partition was especially undesirable in the case of "taxpayer serf" families
because it rendered the resultant smaller households incapable of meet-
ing the kind of feudal obligations and exactions peculiar to serf families
of this sort. The obligations of such families were allocated on a *family*
rather than on an individual basis, and each family division therefore
meant proportionately greater obligation per family member. But most
agricultural serf families in Tibet were "small householders" who, while
less well off than taxpayer serfs, had no comparable reason for avoiding
family division. They did not have family estates which could be passed
from generation to generation. Their feudal obligations were smaller
than those of taxpayer serf families and were allocated on an *individual*
rather than on a family basis. In short, a family division in their case did
not impose greater obligation per person than before partition. It should
come as no surprise, therefore, that most small householder marriages
were monogamous. In the Tibetan case, at least, polyandry was *not* the
result of extreme poverty. Rather it provided a means by which the more
prosperous serf families maintained and improved their social and economic status.

6

Regulation
of Marriage

In many societies custom dictates not only whom one may or may not marry but also whom one ought to or even must marry. Custom may require or encourage people to find a spouse within certain groups (i.e., "endogamously") or to marry outside specific groups (i.e., "exogamously"). The terms "exogamy" and "endogamy" should always be used with respect to a clearly specified group—like a village, village constellation, language group, caste, religious group, or descent group. And it should also be clear as to whether we are referring to marital preferences or to the way in which marriages are actually contracted. There is no expressed preference for Kibbutz exogamy in Israel, for example, but studies of actual marriage patterns have indicated that people who inhabit such communities do tend to marry exogamously (Spiro 1954). Many Americans believe prospective spouses should share a common religion, class, or ethnic identity—that religious, class, and ethnic groups should be more or less endogamous. As we all well know, however, Americans vary in terms of their actual adherence to such a model and many marital boundaries have begun to erode. In some instances new ones have been erected to replace them.

In most of China people express the belief that marriage should be community exogamous. Although the ideal of exogamy is widespread there seems to have been considerable variation in terms of its realization; in some villages people embraced the ideal but married within the community quite frequently. Chinese communities exclusively inhabited by the descendants of a single ancestor are likely to be exogamous in reality as well as in idea, but where communities contain several descent groups the potentiality for endogamous marriage exists. A comparison of Chinese community studies suggests that the ideal of community exogamy is most likely to be compromised in villages with poorly developed descent groups and in which affinal and cross-kin associations are given special emphasis for economic and/or political-military reasons. Even where Chinese conform closely to the ideal of community exogamy we sometimes find that particular constellations of hamlets, villages, or other local units tend to be endogamous, and often these same communities are also involved in cooperative economic, political, ritual, and military endeavors of major importance (see Pasternak, 1972).

Groups formed on the basis of descent from a common ancestor are generally exogamous, at least in principle. There are exceptions, however, as among the Arab Bedouin. Although Arabs trace descent "patrilineally" (i.e., exclusively through males), they believe that a man should marry his father's brother's daughter—a patrilineal relative. We will have more to say about this particular form of cousin marriage shortly; for the present we need only note that while Moslems generally, and Arab Bedouin in particular, believe that the descent group should be endogamous, evidence suggests that conformity to this ideal is variable. In chapter 8 we will study other descent groups in which endogamous marriage occurs and is actually encouraged among people of certain status despite a general belief that the descent group should be exogamous.

Cousin Marriage

Besides providing guidance as to where spouses should be obtained, cultural rules sometimes also encourage marriage with "cousins" of various sorts. Societies may vary in the way in which they terminologically identify cousins, but anthropologists conventionally distinguish two basic types (see Figure 6-1)—"parallel" cousins, related through kinsmen of like sex (i.e., FaBr children and MoSi children), and "cross" cousins who are related through kinsmen of different sex (i.e., FaSi children and MoBr children). For some purposes it is useful to further distinguish cousins in terms of whether they are related to a person (Ego) on his father's (i.e., "patrilateral") or mother's (i.e., "matrilateral") side. It is also important to distinguish between "biological" and "classificatory" cousins. The latter include individuals who, while not actually biologically cousins are

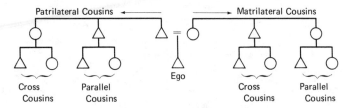

Figure 6-1   Types of Cousins

nevertheless customarily classified (terminologically) with them for certain
purposes.

Table 6-1 reveals some curious differences in the relative frequencies
of cultural preferences for marriage with various kinds of cousins. The
table indicates that although about half of all societies are not favorably
disposed toward marriage with a "cousin," 38 percent of them allow or
even prefer some kind of cousin marriage. Among those permitting such
marriage, moreover, few allow marriage with a parallel cousin; in most
cases only marriage with a cross cousin is tolerated or preferred. Furthermore, although most societies allowing marriage with a cross cousin tend
to prefer a symmetrical arrangement in which a person is free to marry
either a patrilateral or matrilateral cross cousin, it is curious indeed that
where societies allow or prefer only one type of cross cousin they are three

Table 6-1   RULES GOVERNING COUSIN MARRIAGE, BY RELATIVE FREQUENCY
AND RULE OF DESCENT*

Type of Cousin Marriage	Number	Percent	Percent by Rule of Descent			
			Matri	Double	Patri	Bilateral
Pref. for Parallel Cousins	12	2	0	0	5	0
Pref. for Patrilateral Cross Cousins	16	3	10	17	1	1
Pref. for Matrilateral Cross Cousins	49	9	8	17	14	2
Pref. for Symmetrical Cross Cousins	88	16	25	14	18	9
Marriage Permitted with Any First Cousin	45	8	2	0	5	15
Marriage Not Approved With Any First Cousin	277	49	39	48	44	59
No Data Available	77	14	16	3	13	15
Totals	564	100	100	100	100	100

* Based on data in F. W. Moore, *Readings in Cross-Cultural Anthropology* (1961).

times more likely to allow matrilateral cross cousin marriages than marriages with patrilateral cross cousins.

Cross Cousin Marriage

A number of theories have been proposed to account for the fact that some kinds of cousin marriage are found more frequently than others in human societies. One approach to this question requires that we generally view the relative popularity of different behavioral forms in terms of their effects on intergroup relations—on the kinds of alliances they generate. One of the most renowned proponents of the structuralist approach in anthropology, Claude Lévi-Strauss, has suggested, for example, that cross cousin marriage, especially the matrilateral variety, is so common in human society because it promotes social integration by regularizing group interdependencies. Like his theoretical predecessor, Émile Durkheim, Lévi-Strauss (1949) argues that one basic function of all trade and exchange in human society is to promote social solidarity through interdependence. Women constitute the most important and most highly valued commodities that people exchange. Therefore, when they generate and perpetuate alliances the exchange of women assumes special importance and how the exchange is accomplished determines the *kind* of social integration that is achieved.

Consider, for example, the hypothetical case in which two groups of brothers (real or classificatory) exchange their "sisters" (see Figure 6-2). The result of a consistent exchange of this sort is that one's wife is simultaneously one's cousin and, furthermore, that cousin marriage is necessarily symmetrical since one's wife can be *either* a matrilateral (mother's brother's daughter) or patrilateral (father's sister's daughter) cross cousin. We should especially note the absence of functional specialization—A's simultaneously give women to, and receive women from, B's and vice versa. The participating groups become affinally related, but the linkage is presumably not as firm as it might be were a different system of exchange to be adopted because the exchange of women is completed, and

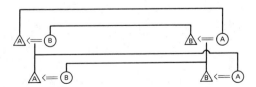

Figure 6-2   Symmetrical Cross Cousin Marriage

balance is achieved, in the space of a single generation. At this point, it is important to observe that the implications of one form of marriage or another with respect to group solidarity can only be presumed since no one, so far as we know, has empirically demonstrated that suggested consequences actually occur.

We observed earlier that marriage is more often tolerated with matrilateral than with patrilateral cross cousins and that matrilateral cross cousin marriage is especially characteristic of patrilineal societies while the patrilateral variant is especially common in matrilineal contexts. One reason suggested for the relative frequency of matrilateral cross cousin marriage is that most of the world's societies are also patrilineal. On the other hand, as Table 6-1 indicates, a unilineal rule of descent is by no means invariably associated with cross cousin marriage; the rule of descent alone does not cause cousin marriage to emerge. In addition, patrilineal societies are actually just as likely to have symmetrical cousin marriage as matrilateral cross cousin marriage, while matrilineal societies prefer symmetrical cross cousins more commonly than patrilateral cross cousins. Lévi-Strauss and others (cf., Needham 1962) have pointed out that matrilateral cross cousin marriage also generates firmer social integration than does its patrilateral counterpart, and for this reason may be more commonly preferred.

Consider a matrilineally organized society in which the preferred mode of residence is avunculocal and the preferred form of marriage is with one's patrilateral cross cousin (see Figure 6-3). Because residence is avunculocal, each local group (A, B, and C) naturally consists of a core of males related through the female line. Notice especially that in each generation the groups exchange women in *opposite* directions. In the first generation B's receive women from A's and give brides to C's, in the next generation

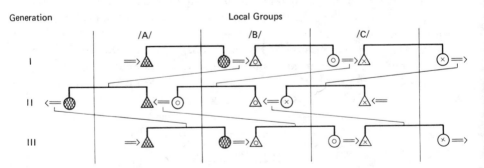

Figure 6-3 Patrilateral Cross Cousin Marriage

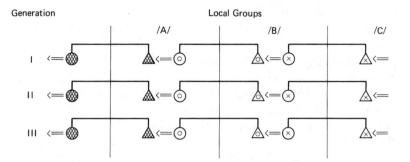

Figure 6-4 Matrilateral Cross Cousin Marriage

the direction of exchange is reversed, and in the third generation the direction is again reversed. A balance of exchange may be achieved among groups in the course of two generations. A patrilateral cross cousin marriage system is like the symmetrical cross cousin system described earlier in that any group is both a giver and receiver of women with respect to another group. Both systems of cousin marriage also generate "mechanical solidarity" (to use Durkheim's term) in the sense that units comprising the exchange system are functionally equivalent and unspecialized—they are all both givers and receivers of women with respect to each other. But, as Lévi-Strauss and others have pointed out, groups can also be integrated "organically," in terms of functionally specialized and therefore dissimilar units. Where groups are of this sort their interdependence is theoretically greater and the system as a whole is presumably more firmly integrated. As Figure 6-4 indicates, a system of marriage based on consistent matrilateral cross cousin marriage results in this kind of integration. Because the patrilineal society presented in the figure has adopted a patrilocal rule of residence every local group consists of a core of men related through males. Men consistently marry their matrilateral cross cousins. If we compare this figure with the preceding one an important difference emerges—consistent matrilateral cross cousin marriage entails specialization of function as between groups. B's always give women to A's but take their wives from C's, and the marriage system as a whole is "organically" integrated. The cycle of exchange is, theoretically, never completed. The development of human society has involved a process of increasing societal complexity, reflected in increasing specialization and interdependence. Consequently, many anthropologists suggest that matrilateral cross cousin marriage may be more common than patrilateral cross cousin marriage precisely because it stimulates better societal integration. In other words, the matrilateral option may have been exercised more commonly because of the selective advantages it conferred in the struggle of societies for survival. ✎

Alternative explanations have been suggested for the relative frequency of matrilateral cross cousin marriage. While it would not be appropriate to involve the reader in a detailed consideration and comparison of all the proposals and counterproposals relevant to this issue, we might consider, for purposes of contrast, two relatively recent and influential psychologically based explanations.

Some years ago, on the basis of observations made in the Trobriand Islands, the British anthropologist, Bronislaw Malinowski, proposed an explanation for the fact that patrilateral cross cousins are so frequently preferred as spouses in societies in which descent is traced exclusively through females (1929: 81). In matrilineal societies, observed Malinowski, an estate is passed by a man to his sister's son. But no man, claimed Malinowski, really wants to pass his property to his nephew; he would rather pass it to his own son. Thus, in matrilineal societies there exists a fundamental conflict between the principle of descent and paternal desire, and patrilateral cross cousin marriage alleviates this contradiction somewhat by allowing a man to pass his estate to his son's son through his sister's son. Figure 6-2 indicates how this is accomplished. Notice that every male in the figure marries a patrilateral cross cousin with the result that a man's grandson is a matrilineal relative and a proper heir after his nephew. As E. R. Leach pointed out (1961: 65), however, Trobriand Islanders more often marry classificatory cross cousins than biological ones. If a man passes his estate not to his biological grandson but rather to a classificatory grandson—to someone he merely refers to as "son's son," then Malinowski's argument is spurious.

More recently, two social scientists, G. Homans and D. M. Schneider (1955), like Malinowski before them, noted the special relationship between matrilateral cross cousin marriage and patrilineal descent on the one hand and patrilateral cross cousin marriage and matrilineal descent on the other, and proposed a psychological basis for the linkage. Their reasoning may be summarized as follows:

In a patrilineal society authority is provided by a father while a mother is considered indulgent. As children grow, sentiments developed with respect to each parent are extended, or generalized, to include the siblings of their parents. Thus, attitudes developed with respect to one's mother are extended to her brother and he too is thought of as a friendly and indulgent figure. Marriage with a matrilateral cross cousin is one expression of the particularly warm relationship between a man and his maternal uncle in patrilineal societies. In matrilineal societies, on the other hand, authority is provided not by a father but by the mother's brother. A maternal uncle is interested in his sister's children because they, and not his own children, are members of his descent group. He must concern himself with the upbringing of his nephews and nieces but he can afford to be quite indulgent toward his own children. The attitudes a child develops with respect to an indulgent father are extended to his paternal aunt and to her children, and marriage with one's patrilateral cross cousin supposedly reflects this "extension of sentiments."•

There are many problems with this interpretation (see R. Needham, 1962).\One of the most important is that it assumes a questionable and certainly unproven psychological process—the extension of sentiments from primary to secondary relatives.•Perhaps one classifies some secondary relatives with primary ones because they are socially or functionally similar in important ways rather than because of some natural, inevitable psychological process.\The theory is also suspiciously male-oriented; are we to suppose that females do not extend sentiments in the same fashion?• If the sexes do not differ in terms of the psychological processes that guide child development, then a female in a matrilineal society should also have a special affinity for *her* patrilateral cross cousin and for *her* matrilateral cross cousin in a patrilineal society; yet she often ends up marrying her matrilateral cross cousin in the former and her patrilateral cross cousin in the latter!\In addition, the extension of sentiments thesis does not enable us to predict the conditions under which the proposed extension will or will not occur, or the conditions under which generalization of sentiments will or will not be associated with cross cousin marriage. Furthermore, as G. P. Murdock has pointed out, most patrilineal societies do not in fact have matrilateral cross cousin marriage and most matrilineal societies lack patrilateral cross cousin marriage (1957: 687).•

After comparing a number of societies in which matrilateral cross cousin marriage is found, E. R. Leach (1961) concluded that this form of marriage has definite and distinctive implications with respect to the kinds of economic and political institutions found in society.\Where we find matrilateral cross cousin marriage, for example, we usually also find local descent groups of *different status.*•Although we cannot, *a priori*, determine whether the givers of women or the receivers are of higher status, we can safely assume there will be a difference between them. If givers of women are senior in one village, furthermore, they will likely be senior in all villages throughout the society. On the basis of his limited comparison of societies\Leach also predicted that status differences expressed by matrilateral cross cousin marriage will be manifested as well in other cultural institutions—the custom often also signals the presence of unequal political and territorial rights.•Where wife givers are socially superior to wife receivers, for example, we can expect their political and territorial rights to be superior as well.\In short, matrilateral cross cousin marriage reflects inequality and is part of a society's political and economic structure. And because matrilateral cross cousin marriage provides an effective mechanism for linking local units of different status in the absence of more complex political mechanisms and institutions, Leach suggests that it is particularly suited to loosely integrated political systems, like those found in feudal societies.

In chapter 3 we discussed some recent cross-cultural research that bears directly on the association between incest regulation and certain genetic and demographic phenomena. The reader may recall Melvin Ember's suggestion (M. Ember n.d.) that, in the course of human development, natural selection probably favored cultural patterns that served to maximize reproductive rates. Because sexual relations between close relatives would have the opposite effect, customs discouraging such relations probably were favored and societies that adopted such customs probably did better in the long run than those that didn't. A custom which extends the incest taboo from primary relatives to first cousins would serve the same purpose, which might explain why so many societies do not allow marriage with cousins.

Parallel Cousin Marriage

We have already observed that parallel cousin marriage is rare in the ethnographic record. One explanation for its relative infrequency is that most of the world's societies organize people into exogamous descent groups, and parallel cousin marriage requires descent group endogamy. In a patrilineal society, for example, a man belongs to the same descent group as his patrilateral parallel cousin; in a matrilineal setting he belongs to the same descent group as his matrilateral parallel cousin. But descent group exogamy would not be violated were a man, in a patrilineal situation, to marry his matrilateral parallel cousin, or to marry his patrilateral parallel cousin in a matrilineal society since these cousins are not members of his descent group. Apart from this we must also account for the few societies in which descent groups are ideally endogamous and parallel cousins are preferred spouses.

A number of social scientists have assumed that parallel cousin marriage functions to keep property intact by locking it within the kinship group (cf., Rosenfeld 1957; Granqvist 1931). The preference for parallel cousin marriage in Arab society, for example, has been attributed by some to the fact that Islamic or Koranic law entitles a daughter to half the inheritance of a son. If a man marries his daughter to his brother's son, goes the argument, he can at least ensure that her inheritance will remain

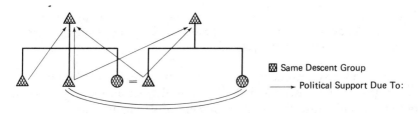

☒ Same Descent Group

⟶ Political Support Due To:

Figure 6-5 Parallel Cousin Marriage, Descent, and Political Support

within his own descent group. But this explanation for parallel cousin preference is not really entirely convincing. For one thing, as F. Barth (1954: 170) pointed out, it assumes that people actually regulate their behavior in terms of Koranic law and provide daughters with half the inheritance of a son. In fact, this is not invariably the case and, as Murphy and Kasdan (1959: 17) observed, why should people concern themselves with what daughters may carry off at marriage in any case—is it not possible that a family or descent group can more than compensate their loss by bringing in a daughter-in-law with an even more substantial inheritance! If parallel cousin marriage is really so effective a way to keep property intact, moreover, why do so few of the world's peoples employ this technique for doing so?

Barth suggests that parallel cousin marriage, at least among the Kurds, played an important role in "solidifying the minimal lineage as a corporate group in factional struggle" (1954: 171). A man is willing to forego the brideprice normally expected for a daughter in order to acquire something of greater value—the complete political support of his nephew. In short, an ambitious man may use parallel cousin marriage to solidify, politically, his close patrilineal relatives (see Figure 6-5). The thrust of Barth's interpretation was that, because it reduced the likelihood of conflict within the descent group, parallel cousin marriage enhanced the group's ability to counter threats from outside.

Murphy and Kasdan (1959) have proposed an explanation for parallel cousin marriage among the Arab Bedouin that also focuses upon its political functions, but their emphasis is not so much on the integrating effects of parallel cousin marriage as on its contribution to the "extreme fission process" characteristic of and essential to Bedouin society. In their view, successful expansion of the Bedouin has been accomplished in part as a result of their ability to split and consolidate as situations required. Murphy and Kasdan therefore proposed that,

> while consolidation of wealth, or of power, may constitute a motivation for those who wish to marry their father's brother's daughter, one structural function of the institution is to promote the segmenta-

tion process. From this point of view, feud and fission are not at all dysfunctional factors but are necessary to the persistence and viability of Bedouin society (1959: 18).

We have already seen how cross cousin marriage can generate alliances among groups. A consistent pattern of parallel cousin marriage has the opposite effect—it discourages development of strong and permanent alliances either within or between descent groups. While parallel cousin marriage may indeed contribute to the *temporary* unity of a group of closely related individuals it also functions to inhibit formation and perpetuation of more inclusive corporate descent groups. Notice that parallel cousin marriage during the first two generations in Figure 6-6 joins the progeny of

Generation

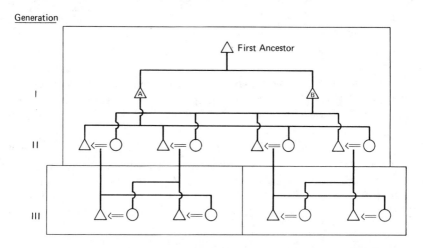

Figure 6-6   The Effect of Parallel Cousin Marriage in Bedouin Society

A and B in terms of affinal as well as agnatic bonds. For two generations parallel cousin marriage contributes to the unity and interdependence of the descent group. In the third generation, however, the result of this marriage pattern is that the agnatic group splits into two endogamous subgroups, each of which becomes an independent and politically coherent minimal descent group. In this sense Arab Bedouin society lacks bounded and stable descent groups. Although some anthropologists (e.g., Fortes 1953; Murdock 1949) have proposed that the *raison-d'être* of unilineal descent groups is to define discrete, clearly bounded, and countinuing corporate groups the Bedouin data indicates that if unilineal descent groups are endogamous, no "isolable, discrete kin groups are found." As Murphy and Kasdan put it,

> in societies having exogamous descent groups the boundaries and membership of the group are clearly set by stipulating marriage outside of it; descent groups among the Bedouin have no such clear-cut means of definition. Rather, the internal logic of the system extends agnatic ties in decreasing degree to all members of Arab society (1959: 27).

We have not yet arrived at a satisfactory explanation for parallel cousin marriage. Most attempts to account for it have been functional in nature —they highlight the adaptive advantages of such marriage under specific circumstances. But even if we grant that parallel cousin marriage performs the functions some anthropologists have attributed to it (and there are arguments even here), we are nonetheless still unable to account for the fact that so few of the world's societies employ this device and we are unable to specify the conditions under which these functions are likely to be performed in this particular fashion rather than in some alternative way. These questions remain unanswered for the present.

Marriage by the Section

Wherever a society is divided into two exogamous groups or divisions anthropologists conventionally refer to them as "moieties." Robin Fox (1967) has suggested that moieties may have originated in a regular marital exchange between two local groups—two groups of "brothers" exchanged their "sisters." As population grew the original groups segmented. While the number of local groups increased the original two-group identity was maintained in the form of exogamous moieties, each consisting of a number of discrete local groups. Such moieties may have been named after natural phenomena or after places of origin, and they may sometimes have been involved in reciprocal ritual or other functions. The males of one moiety continued to be "brothers," and to find their spouses among the "sisters" of their counterparts in the opposite moiety. Such a marriage system is sometimes referred to as a "Kariera" system, after a people aboriginal to Australia who practice it. As Figure 6-7 indicates, the structural consequences of this moiety arrangement is that any Ego ultimately marries a cross cousin. Since there are a number of groups in each moiety, however, the fact that Ego marries a cross cousin does not necessarily mean he marries a biological cross cousin. A "cross

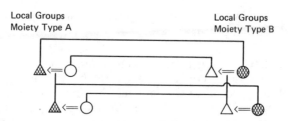

Figure 6-7   Structural Consequences of Moiety Exchange
Between Two Sets of "Siblings"

cousin" is rather a girl of appropriate generation from a group of opposite
moiety. The social world of any Ego in such a system effectively comprises four named categories of females, which is why it is often also
referred to by anthropologists as a "four class" or "four section" system
(see Table 6-2).

Table 6-2   A FOUR SECTION MARRIAGE SYSTEM

Named Section	Ego's Generation	Ego's Moiety
1	Yes	Yes
2	No	Yes
3*	Yes	No
4	No	No

* Only females in this class are marriageable

In the four class system a man must marry a woman of his own generation but of opposite moiety, and when he refers to a woman by the term
appropriate to a cross cousin he may be indicating little more than that
she is a "marriageable woman." A simple model may further clarify what
is involved in a four class or four section marriage system. Imagine a
hypothetical patrilineal society consisting of two named moieties, "Peg"
and "Hole." Alternate generations in both moieties are also alternatively
named "Square" and "Round." Thus, the son of a Square Peg is a Round
Peg and the son of a Square Hole is a Round Hole. If we apply a simple
rule that a man must marry a girl of his own generation but of opposite
moiety, then:

Generation/Moiety   Generation/Moiety

Square-Peg ══════════ Square-Hole

Round-Peg ══════════ Round-Hole

As anyone in our hypothetical society would quickly point out, any attempt to combine a Square-Peg with a Round-Hole would be inappropriate and ill-advised.

It is characteristic of the Kariera, or four section marriage system, that a man obtains his spouse from a group of the same type as that from which his mother was drawn, and people he refers to as "sisters" are given to such groups. The Aranda, another people aboriginal to Australia, impose a further restriction. They additionally require that a wife not be taken from the same type group as that from which one's mother was obtained; she should come from a group like that from which one's grandmother was taken. This added requirement produces what anthropologists refer to as the "Aranda," "Eight Class," or "Eight Section" marriage system. In this system a man's universe consists not of four but of eight named types of females, only one of which is marriageable (see Table 6-3).

Table 6-3   An Eight Section Marriage System

Named Section	Ego's Generation	Ego's Moiety	Local Group Type A (like mother's)
1	Yes	Yes	Yes
2	Yes	Yes	No
3	No	Yes	Yes
4	No	Yes	No
5	Yes	No	Yes
6*	Yes	No	No
7	No	No	Yes
8	No	No	No

* Only this type female is marriageable

As Figure 6-8 indicates, the structural consequences of the additional requirement imposed in an Eight Section system is that, whether he intends it or not, a man marries someone he classifies as his "patrilateral cross cousin." Anthropologists still do not understand why he is not allowed to take a spouse from the same type group as his father, but Robin Fox has speculated that this kind of marriage system may,

> be a response to a growth in population or the amalgamation of a number of tribes or bands, or anything that increased the numbers of "alliance units." It preserves the moiety system, but brings a larger number of clans into alliance relationships (1967: 198).

The requirement that a man take his wife from a group different from that from which his mother was taken effectively widens a group's affinal

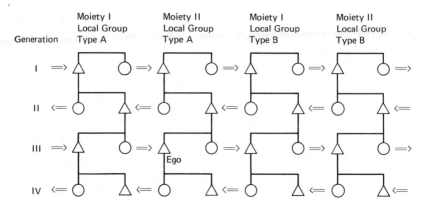

Figure 6-8   The "Aranda" or "Eight Section" Marriage System

network (i.e., the number of groups with which it has relations through marriage) Fox assumes that the proliferation of groups is causal, but he does not explain why, even assuming such a demographic situation, there should be any premium on widely ramifying affinal ties.

In a recent study, A. A. Yengoyan (1968) proposed a relationship between number of sections and demographic factors. Yengoyan found that Australian tribes characterized by subsections (i.e., by Eight Class systems) possess the largest areas and population sizes, but have the lowest population densities. As the number of sections decrease, so do tribal areas and sizes. Population density, on the other hand, goes up (1968: 194). Yengoyan calculates that the more sections a people employ the greater the population there must be since,

> when moiety restrictions are imposed the number of potential mates, and possibly potential competitors, is reduced by one-half. Subsequently, with section marriage restrictions, the number of eligible females is reduced to one-fourth of the "O" condition, and with subsection marriage to one-eighth (1968: 195).

Thus, population size (which in turn responds to ecological and environmental factors) is an important determinant of whether a people *can actually practice*, or marry in terms of, various section systems; realization of an Eight Section ideal requires a greater breeding population than a Four Section ideal (cf., Yengoyan 1968 and Meggitt 1968).

A number of scholars have suggested that section systems may in fact not be directly or primarily involved in the regulation of marriage (cf., Service 1960c, Meggitt 1968, and Yengoyan 1968). As Elman Service put it, these systems may actually "have to do with social behavior and not merely the regulation of marriage" (1960c: 433; cf., Meggitt 1968: 179–81).

Commenting on the relationship between tribal area, population density, and number of sections, Yengoyan observes that Eight Section systems are usually found in areas of Australia where groups meet relatively infrequently because they are widely spaced. Under such circumstances,

> expansion of section terms not only combines spatially distant groups into meaningful units for marriage and ceremonial functions, but also permits reciprocal movements of related groups into larger territorial domains. . . . In aboriginal Australia, one may regard the interlocking of kinsmen through section and subsection groupings as allowing for greater interaction and mobility over exploitable lands and thus "insuring" utilizable resources (1968: 199; cf., Service 1960: 431).

Although Fox and Yengoyan highlight conditions under which section systems of various sorts are likely to be realized and persist, neither of them has really explained how section systems emerge in the first place. The fact that they may constitute one response to certain environmental and ecological conditions does not mean alternative solutions are not possible; indeed, were alternative mechanisms not available we would surely find section systems more widespread in the world. What has still to be determined, therefore, are the conditions under which section systems of various sorts are most likely to emerge.

7

The Family

Kinship relationships of which families are formed are fundamental to human societies. No matter how they conceive of relatedness, human beings everywhere recognize kinship and use it as a basis for defining the content of relationships between people and very often as a basis for forming social groups. Similarly, the legitimization of children, rights in children, and an exchange of sexual and other rights are nearly everywhere associated with unions between men and women. It follows from the universality of kinship and the near universality of marriage, that, by definition, family relationships are nearly universal (Bender 1971: 238).

We have discussed incest regulation, rules of postmarital residence, and some of the customs that people have devised to regulate marriage. In this chapter we turn to the "family;" we consider its definition and possible origins, the forms it may take, and the conditions that might encourage one form of the family rather than another.

Definition and Foundations of the Family

Although most anthropologists assume that families are somehow necessary and are therefore found in all human societies, there is little agreement about how the family originated. Ralph Linton suggested that "conjugal" families (i.e., those consisting of a husband, wife, and their children if any) are everywhere based upon "an assumption of continuity in the mated relationship" (1968: 280). He further proposed that a combination of two physiological factors may underlie this stable mated relationship—male dominance and the constancy of human sexual interest. There are no clearly defined mating seasons among humans and males are everywhere dominant as a result of the natural differences in size and vigor as between the sexes. As Linton states,

> even the earliest men were able to keep particular women to themselves and to prevent these women from bestowing their favors on other men, at least as long as their husbands were present (1968: 281).

There are some problems, however, with Linton's proposal. As we noted in the introduction to this book some of our closest primate relatives fail to display the fierce jealousy that Linton attributes to early man. Some nonhuman primates have clearly defined mating seasons but nevertheless tolerate adultery and maintain stable mated relationships. Some clearly enjoy stable mated relationships without being either constantly sexy or jealous, and if we could better understand why these animals remain together we might shed some light on the foundation of human mated relationships as well. Humans could maintain such relationships for very distinctive and unique reasons, of course, but what we now know about nonhuman primate behavior should at least cause us to hesitate before accepting Linton's speculation on the origins of the stable mated relationship and the conjugal family.

Linton also suggested a number of secondary factors that might have served to encourage and bolster stable mated relationships among earliest humans. Men and women have a basic need for security and companionship—psychological needs that Linton proposed are probably best satisfied by a long-term association. The "universal division of labor by sex" similarly serves to integrate partners and some anthropologists have even suggested that this is *the* basic reason for the stable mated relationship. We should be troubled, however, by the fact that some nonhuman primates enjoy stable mated relationships in the absence of any obvious division of labor by sex; in most instances each animal eats what it collects and food sharing, except between mother and infant, is minimal.

Another difficulty with Linton's discussion of the family and its origins was that he attempted to account for the family in terms of certain presumably universal functions. Particular functions, however, can usually be performed by different social forms (Goldschmidt 1966). As Donald Bender observed, there is no question but that there are certain necessarily recurring daily activities such as sleeping, eating, and child care which must be carried out. The point to be made is that while these activities are conveniently carried out by families and/or households, they need not be carried out by either (1971: 239).

We must therefore explain why it is that people have so often employed the family as the device for performing suggested functions.

The writings of G. P. Murdock reveal a similarly functional view of the family.

> The family is a social group characterized by common residence, economic cooperation, and reproduction. It includes adults of both sexes, at least two of whom maintain a socially approved sexual relationship, and one or more children, own or adopted, of the sexually cohabiting adults (1949: 1).

Just as there were ethnographic instances that defied a definition of marriage, there are a number of cases which complicate any attempt to formulate a final, all-embracing definition of the family. Murdock's definition is certainly not the only one the scholarly world has known or employed but it will serve as a starting point for our discussion of the difficulties inherent in any attempt to arrive at a definition that will satisfy all observers and situations. One of the most serious shortcomings with Murdock's definition is its requirement that there be common residence. This forces us to exclude all cases in which husband and wife live separately as well as instances in which children live apart from their parents. To require that members of a family live together is, in effect, to confuse qualitatively different social units—the family and the household (cf., de Gonzáles 1965; Bender 1967, 1971; Vicary 1967; and Goode 1967).

When he examined a sample of the world's societies Murdock found three distinct forms of the family as he defined it. Some societies had only nuclear families, consisting of a married couple and their offspring (the equivalent of Linton's conjugal family). In others there were also polygamous families, containing two or more nuclear units affiliated by plural marriage, or extended families, in which two or more nuclear families are affiliated through an extension of the parent-child relationship or the sibling relationship rather than by plural marriage. It is unfortunate that Murdock didn't stress the difference between these "stem" and "joint" form extended families since, as will be argued below, they probably differ significantly in terms of their internal dynamics and stability. Throughout this chapter we will reserve the prefix "joint" for families that minimally consist of two or more married siblings. If a family is larger than nuclear but does not meet the definitional requirement for a joint family we will call it a "stem" family (cf., Lang 1946: 14–15).

After comparing 250 of the world's societies Murdock concluded that the nuclear family exists as a "distinct and strongly functional group in every society" and that it is universal because it everywhere performs four functions essential to human life—a sexual function, a reproductive function, an economic function, and an educational or socializing function. Let us consider these functions individually.

Although the nuclear family does provide an institutionalized way for people to satisfy their continuous sexual needs and appetites, there are societies in which premarital or postmarital sexual license is allowed or encouraged and in some cases sexual relations may even be employed to reinforce nonconjugal relationships. The need for sexual gratification certainly cannot be considered the primary force driving people into stable mated relationships. Sexual gratification can be a reward of family life without being its cause. As Murdock himself observed:

> In view of the frequency with which sexual relationships are permitted outside of marriage, it would seem the part of scientific caution to assume merely that sex is an important but not the exclusive factor in maintaining the marital relationship within the nuclear family, and to look elsewhere for auxiliary support (1949: 6–7).

Murdock says that auxiliary support is provided by a family's economic function. Because "a man and a woman make an exceptionally efficient cooperating unit," claims Murdock, "all known human societies have developed specialization and cooperation between the sexes" (1949: 7). But, as we noted in our discussion of nonhuman primates, a number of species form units like our family in the absence of any clear economic division of labor between the sexes. As Murdock admitted, furthermore, the economic function like the sexual function cannot alone account for the emergence or universality of the family:

> Sexual unions without economic cooperation are common, and there are relationships between men and women involving a division of labor without sexual gratification, e.g., between brother and sister, master and maidservant, or employer and secretary, (1949: 8).

Murdock proposes that the nuclear family is "universal and inevitable" because it everywhere performs certain essential functions even though two of them, the sexual and the economic functions, could admittedly be performed outside the family and, indeed, sometimes actually are. Only when *both* functions are combined do we have "marriage," according to

Murdock, and only when we have marriage do we have the "family" (1949: 8). We are thus confronted by an assertion that because the family is universal so is marriage since families cannot exist without marriage. Family and marriage everywhere exist, therefore, to perform both the sexual and economic functions. But if the sexual and economic functions could be performed in other ways why then should marriage be universal and the family inevitable?

Murdock proposed that the reproductive and socializing functions of the family provide important additional support. As many anthropologists have pointed out, however, only the mother-child relationship really need endure once successful implantation has been accomplished (see, for example, Adams 1960: 41). A husband, like the drone bee, is dispensable. Indeed, as we have seen, a Nayar male does not live with the mother of his children. The Nayar clearly lack nuclear families since there is no permanently attached husband; a woman lives with her sisters and one of her brothers and enjoys the attentions of a variety of husbands who share sexual relations with her but who do not eat, live, work, or perform a socializing function in her family unit. There is no married couple that constitutes a legal, productive, distributive, residential, socializing, or consuming unit. In short, there is no nuclear unit to perform any of the four functions that Murdock suggests are essential to the family (Gough 1968; cf., Spiro 1954: 839–846; Solien de Gonzáles 1965; and Otterbein 1965, 1970).

Murdock's insistence that "the burden of education and socialization everywhere falls primarily upon the nuclear family" (1949: 10) is supported by other writers, some of whom even propose that it is this function in particular that requires the existence of a family in all societies. They argue that only socialization requires small units for effective implementation and only small kin-organized units are capable of effectively performing this function. For example, M. J. Levy and L. A. Fallers have written,

> Let us assume, then, that small, kinship-structured units are universal—are indeed structural requisites of any society. Functionally, socialization would appear to be the heart of the matter. Parsons and Bales have argued with great cogency that socialization requires small units and that completely non-kinship-structured small units are unlikely to carry out the functions effectively (although of course human ingenuity may devise alternatives). Of the other "universal functions" attributed by Murdock to the family, reproduction and sexual regulation would appear to be associated with, and probably secondary to, socialization. . . . It is not so much that families universally fulfill economic functions vis-à-vis other units and the society at large; clearly, the degree to which and the ways in which they do so are subject to enormous variation. Rather, the point would

seem to be that families, like other social units, must make provision
for the distribution of goods and services—that, like other units, they
have economic aspects (1959: 648; cf., Parsons 1955).

But even if we assume that small, kinship-structured units are needed in
any society, and even if we assume that they always perform a socializing
function, it does not follow that there is only one kind of small, kinship-
structured unit which everywhere carries out each aspect or phase of the
socialization process. As Levy and Fallers observed (1959: 648–651), different aspects or phases of the socialization process may be performed by
different small, kinship-structured units at various times. There are docu-
mented instances in which the major burden of socialization has even
been born by non-kin—on some communes and kibbutzim, for example
(see Spiro 1954; cf., Bender 1967: 503 and 1971: 239). Nor does it follow
that the minimal family unit in every society necessarily corresponds to
a nuclear family. Where marriages are polygamous or families extended
the family need not simply comprise an aggregation of nuclear units.
There may be unmarried siblings, surviving parents, or other kinds of
relatives present and the entire family often participates in socializing
the young. It is for these reasons that Levy and Fallers propose a more
general definition of the family:

> We suggest that the concept "family," to be useful for general com-
> parative purposes, should be used to refer not to a single social unit
> in each society, but rather to any small, kinship-structured unit
> which carries out aspects of the relevant functions (1959: 650).

The problem of defining the family has by no means been resolved to
the satisfaction of all. My own inclination is to view the family as the
minimal corporate, or property-owning kin group in any society. As was
suggested earlier in connection with marriage, however, lack of consensus
should not deter us from accepting some explicit working definition of the
family for the purpose of relating family, however it is defined, to other
phenomena.

Factors Contributing to Variation in Family Form

Many anthropologists have discussed the relationship between family
form and level of societal development. A view that is currently very
popular is that the relationship is curvilinear—that is, that the most likely
place for an emergence and persistence of extended families is at the
intermediate levels of societal complexity (see Figure 7-1). A number of
cross-cultural studies provide statistical support for this belief; they show

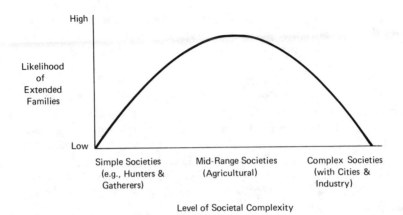

Figure 7-1 A Current View of the Relationship Between Extended
Families and Level of Societal Complexity

an association between hunting and independent families, a rise in the
frequency of extended families in agricultural settings, and a decline in
their frequency in the most complex (urban-industrial) societies (cf., Blumberg and Winch 1972; Nimkoff and Middleton 1960).

There is a relationship between agriculture and a tolerance for extended
families but the reasons for the fit are not yet clearly understood. One
explanation for the frequency of extended families in agricultural societies, proposed by Nimkoff and Middleton (1960), is that such contexts
provide a larger and more stable food supply than hunting and gathering
settings and can therefore support such families. In addition, agriculture
imposes a greater demand for family labor and a better basis for the
development of private property.

The notion that hunters and gatherers live from hand to mouth is
commonplace in anthropological literature; it has generally been assumed
that people at this socio-cultural level must live in this fashion (and
have always done so) because their technology is relatively unproductive.
Nimkoff and Middleton suggest that "participation of many persons in
seed-and root-gathering generally not only fails to increase the per capita
harvest but decreases it" (1960: 218). But recent studies already demonstrate that foraging can provide support for multifamily groupings among
nonhuman primates (cf., Kummer 1971). Studies now available also suggest that hunting-gathering technology may be more productive than previously believed even in the most marginal of environments and that
people at this level of development can enjoy considerable leisure and
also support multifamily groupings (cf., Lee 1969 and Woodburn 1968a,
1968b). There are also studies which indicate that the increased produc-

tion made possible by agriculture does not necessarily produce either better fed or more consistently fed producers (cf., Harris 1959; Gross 1971; Woodburn 1968a; and Lee 1969). The benefits of increased productivity are not invariably shared with the producers; in many instances they are siphoned off by landlords and tax-collectors who press the producers for still greater productivity. It is quite possible that paleolithic hunters and gatherers, not confined to inhospitable environments, might have enjoyed even more impressive productive capacity than their contemporary counterparts. If hunters and gatherers do not have extended families it is probably *not* because their form of subsistence cannot sustain them but rather because other types of multifamily groupings are preferable for some reason. Among hunting-gathering peoples, as among non-human primates, multifamily groupings are adaptive in most instances—they are useful in locating food, in warning and defending against dangers and, in the case of humans, they are effective mechanisms for the storage of essential food resources through sharing. If multifamily groups or bands do not consist of extended families it may be because tensions generated within such families render them unstable.

My own suspicion is that joint families are relatively rare and more difficult to maintain than stem or nuclear families (even in societies that prize them) because the strains and stresses inherent in them are greater. If hunters and gatherers do not often have joint families it is probably not because they could not sustain them in terms of their productive resources and capabilities but rather because there is no need to suppress family partition. Why should they endure a relatively permanent association between consanguineously related units if group functions could be performed as well or better by unrelated and highly mobile family units of a more simple type? Given the techno-environmental constraints upon many contemporary hunter-gatherers, and their propensity for nomadism, advantages are to be obtained from any customs and practices that maximize their ability to migrate, aggregate, and disperse as conditions require, and extended families might provide less flexibility than nuclear families under such circumstances (cf., Woodburn 1968b). The rarity of extended families among contemporary hunting-gathering peoples may also be a funtion of demographic factors—especially the character of their child-spacing mechanisms (see Sussman 1972). There might be fewer extended families among contemporary hunter-gatherers than among sedentary peoples if they produce fewer children and if fewer of their children achieve adulthood.

Nimkoff and Middleton suggest that the greater tolerance for extended families among agriculturalists is probably related to their ownership of property, especially land:

If division results in many small pieces, each member of the family owning and working his own piece, the system becomes relatively unproductive. There is a disposition under the circumstances to hold the family land intact and to add to it if possible (1960. 220).

Property is probably in some way related to the higher propensity that cultivators have for extended families; it is also likely that people with land are normally reluctant to divide it. But the economic disadvantages of land division may be easier to endure than rising intrafamilial tensions, especially where alternative means exist to maintain or even to increase yield levels after family and land partition. Indeed, yields per unit area have been growing in many regions of Asia despite land fragmentation and a general decrease in cultivable area. Farmers may work harder, apply fertilizers and irrigation more effectively, or plant improved varieties of seed or more profitable crops. The ethnographic record contains ample evidence that joint families can thrive on relatively small parcels of land. The size of a cultivated holding is not the only factor determining manpower need—much depends on the crops being grown, watering conditions, and the nature of other family enterprises and investments.

Recent studies by M. Cohen (1967, 1968, and 1970) indicate how choice of crop can affect family form. In one rural Taiwanese community Cohen found an unusually high frequency of joint families. Such families were especially common among farmers cultivating tobacco (46 percent of all tobacco-growing families), but were relatively rare among farmers engaged in the cultivation of other crops (only 16 percent of such families). Cohen suggests that the difference between the two groups had to do with the relatively greater and more constant labor requirements of tobacco production. Because female labor is especially required, anything that diverts women from tobacco production is economically disadvantageous. Since each family partition produces discrete domestic units, with separate sets of domestic chores, family division should be avoided if possible. Cohen demonstrates how the reallocation of labor required by a family partition has the effect of reducing income derived from tobacco (Cohen 1968: 176).

On the basis of their comparison of cases in the *Ethnographic Atlas* (Murdock 1967), Blumberg and Winch (1972) suggested that extended families are most likely to be formed and to persist in societies characterized by extensive agriculture or horticulture and in societies characterized by intensive agriculture on permanent fields. The frequency of such families reportedly drops off in agricultural settings once irrigation has been introduced (1972: 906–7; cf., Orenstein 1956). My own research on Taiwan (1972a, 1972b) suggested that the frequency of complex families may precipitously decline with the introduction of canal irrigation because the requirements of cultivation no longer require families to prepare and

plant private plots simultaneously. Where cultivation is largely or exclusively rainfall dependent, and where rainfall is unreliable, a family may
be under special pressure to prepare its landholdings as soon as onset of
the rains permit and they may therefore be less likely to involve themselves in interfamilial labor exchanges that could delay the planting of
family fields. If most families in an area are under similar pressure, then
labor can be in short supply at critical points in the agricultural cycle
and the cost of hired labor would also be very high. Under such circumstances it would make good sense to rely as much as possible on the
family itself for labor and to suppress centrifugal tendencies within the
family. Rainfall dependence might thus encourage formation and perpetuation of extended families because the emotional advantages to be
derived from a family partition are outweighed by the practical economic
advantages of staying together. Once irrigation replaces a dependence on
rainfall, however, there is more room for interfamilial cooperation simply
because the water supply is more reliable and controllable. Since water
can now be stored and channeled as necessary, families are no longer
under the same pressure to act simultaneously and the disadvantages of
family partition are considerably reduced.

Nimkoff and Middleton proposed that agricultural families may try to
"stretch" themselves by adding new members in order to cultivate more
land (1960: 220). But the reverse may actually be the case—namely, that
because a family is cultivating more land it is capable of expanding itself.
And even where landholdings are undivided and rising yields can be
generated on the basis of increased labor, why does such labor have to
come from a single family or household? The ethnographic literature is
filled with examples of interfamilial cooperation and exchange in agriculture. The question therefore remains—under what circumstances will
a family opt to remain undivided rather than partition and obtain labor
and other necessary inputs from other families or in the open market?
Given a demographic and economic capacity for family extension we
must still determine the conditions under which such potentialities are
likely to be realized.

Extended families are also quite common in pastoral societies where
advantages can often be obtained from cooperation in the herding of
animals (see Blumberg and Winch 1972: 914–15). Differences in the frequency, form, and composition of extended families in such societies also
seem to result from economic and environmental factors. The Jie and
Turkana pastoralists of East Africa provide examples (Gulliver 1968a,
1968b). Originally one people, in adapting to different habitats they
developed rather different family organizations. The Jie live under more
favorable environmental conditions than the Turkana, and are able to
supplement transhumant pastoralism with horticulture and to maintain

permanent settlements. The typical Jie "homestead" contains a group of men descended from a single grandfather, together with their wives, sons, sons' wives and children, and unmarried sisters and daughters (1968a: 328). Homesteads in turn consist of "houses," groups of full brothers which are the main stock-owning units in Jie society. While neither homesteads nor houses are free of centrifugal tendencies and pressures (1968a: 330–31), there are counterpressures that effectively delay partition in both cases. For example,

> a house cannot normally afford to exist quite independently: few houses have the resources to make up a full bridewealth; hence, although other kinsmen are asked for help, it is to near agnates in other houses that men look first (Gulliver 1968a: 331).

Cooperation relating to marriage is not the only force that binds agnatically related houses. The members of Jie houses also assist one another in the management of livestock and in other ways (1968a: 332). As Gulliver explains it,

> what is of practical importance . . . is the pattern of continuous cooperation, common residence in the homestead, relatively heavy commitment to mutual assistance in livestock, and the everyday contacts and interests that exist between the various houses. . . . There is usually a good deal of pastoral cooperation, for relatively few houses have both enough animals and enough youths and young men to tend them so that they can be entirely independent in day-to-day management (1968a: 332).

Several Jie homesteads constitute a "clan-hamlet" and several such hamlets form a "settlement." Several settlements in turn make up a "district," and seven districts constitute the Jie "tribe." Ritual activities and an active age-group system function to integrate the various social units that comprise Jie tribal society. In contrast to the Jie, the Turkana live in units that are relatively mobile and changing in composition (Gulliver 1968b: 346). It is the nature of environmental conditions, especially the unpredictable nature of vegetation, that encourages an ideology of independence and a pastoral economy based upon scattered and thinly distributed herds and social groups (1968b: 348–49; see also 356–58). The Turkana, like the Jie, have joint families but they are not coresidential units and they appear to be more prone to fission than those of the Jie (1968b: 356–57). Environmental conditions require that different animals be herded in different locations and, as a result, each joint family is composed of at least two discrete and relatively independent homesteads, neither of which can afford to manage herds of great size because that would require more frequent movement to compensate for a more rapid exhaustion of sparse local vegetation (1968b: 349). Techno-environmental factors apparently select for impermanent kin and cross-kin alliances among the Turkana, and there are fewer incentives in their cases for the formation of enduring social units at any societal level. According to Gulliver,

> an underlying theme of Turkana social organization is the general difficulty of group activity on any large scale because of ecological conditions which cause a widespread dispersal of population together with diverse and frequent movement. Density of population is low everywhere, and in addition there is the cultural norm of strong individualism in connection with nomadic movements so that residential relations seldom become important over a period; and there is neither particular need nor opportunity for the frequent assembly of kinsmen (1968b: 358; see also 351).

Whereas the Turkana live under conditions that encourage the impermanence of social groups at all levels, the Jie are able to support relatively stable social units at a number of levels. Members of the Jie joint family apparently stay together because they need each other, although it is not entirely clear from Gulliver's description why mutual assistance could not be based upon the cooperation of unrelated nuclear families.

Nimkoff and Middleton note an interesting connection between a propensity for extended families and stratification (1960: 220). Not only does the tendency to form extended families increase with the degree of stratification, but,

> even when the subsistence pattern is partialed out as a factor, there continues to be a striking difference between those societies with a relatively little and those with a relatively great degree of social stratification (1960: 220; cf., Blumberg and Winch 1972).

In a similar vein, Clinget and Sween (1974), comparing family organization and family composition in two African cities, discovered that the households with the largest number of children were those headed by individuals who:

> are married to three wives and more, enjoy a high level of educational attainment, perform a modern occupational role, have been previously exposed to modernizing experiences in their migratory history, and have access to modern and spacious housing facilities (1974: 237).

The implication of Nimkoff and Middleton's findings and those of Clinget and Sween is that the connection between stratification and family extension may not necessarily depend on the amount of land a family *cultivates* as much as on other correlates of wealth. Nimkoff and Middleton note that, in the case of India,

> the upper castes, which own more property—especially land—than the lower, have more joint families, whereas the very poor out-castes have the largest proportion of independent families (1960: 220).

Notice that the authors are talking about *landownership* rather than landholding. One can own vast areas of land without cultivating an inch just as one can cultivate large areas of land without owning any. If upper caste Indian families are renting out most or all of their land, then their agricultural enterprises do not involve the kinds of labor that Nimkoff and Middleton suggest are so important a stimulus to family extension. In fact, the association between stratification and extended family may not involve either large landholdings or large landownings; other economic characteristics of upper class status may be of greater importance. We may discover that it is not wealth per se that makes the difference as much as the way in which it is invested. Wealth may be maintained and increased most effectively where it can be channelel into multi-enterprise investments. In commercial-agricultural societies it becomes possible to avoid keeping all eggs in a single basket by investing in more than one economic enterprise and, as several writers have demonstrated (cf., Cohen 1967, 1968, 1970; and Strickon 1962), families can sometimes conserve or increase their wealth more effectively by remaining together and shifting resources around, internally, from enterprise to enterprise than by splitting up and depending on outsiders for required economic inputs. The suppression of fissive tendencies might be especially advantageous where credit sources are poorly developed or where other critical economic resources have to be conserved and kept fluid. The extended family provides one way to weather fluctuations in labor availability, labor cost, crop yield, capital and credit, etc. If this is true, then we might expect such families to be especially frequent where a strong development of private property is combined with frequent fluctuations in critical economic and productive resources. In a stratified commercial-agricultural society the rich can profit from persistence of the joint family in their effort to maintain or to increase the wealth they have accumulated. For precisely the same reasons the very poor might also stand to profit from a suppression of fissive inclinations within the family. Indeed this may explain the association noted by Harumi Befu (1968) between large families in Nakagiri, Japan, and impoverishment. Befu claimed that large families were adaptive given poverty and near starvation subsistence levels:

> In the condition of Nakagiri where people were near the starvation level, it is understandable that there would be unusually great pressure to reduce per capita expenses through coresidence. Under a relatively static demographic condition such as obtained in Nakagiri in the first half of the last century, this situation would tend to inhibit creation of branch households, since branching would divide a household into two smaller units, neither of which would be as well adapted for survival as the original large household. Neither, moreover, would be likely to increase to the original size (1968: 313–14).

It was the need to conserve or maximize resources that made the difference in Nakagiri, but Befu also drew attention to the importance of fluctuations in both yield and critical productive resources (1968: 314), and it may be that agriculture is generally more susceptible to such fluctuations than either hunting-gathering or fishing, which would also contribute to a higher frequency of extended families among agriculturalists. Another example of family extension in response to extreme poverty is found in a commercial setting from Peru (Hammel 1961). This instance introduces a peculiar variant—a household consisting of several independent units that are not necessarily all related:

> A large number of the young independent families in the slum, therefore, are not nuclear, but are laterally extended, including other wage-earning adults who can relieve those economic burdens which are relatively constant for a household group, regardless of its size (rent, water, fuel) and who can occasionally care for children so that mothers and young children can themselves earn extra income (1961: 1001).

Hammel observes that sibling solidarity is especially evident in the slum, where "the sibling group is the only kin group for many immigrants" (1961: 1004).

The findings of Hammel and Befu provide support for Cohen's proposition that the real key to perpetuation of the joint family probably lies in the "interpendent nature of the various economic activities undertaken by different family members." More specifically, Cohen suggested that the joint family is likely to be retained where, in the event of family partition, "the limited possibilities remaining to each unit would not bring total returns as great as those derived from the total investments of the family as now constituted," or where "division would also mean a reduction in total income from present enterprises" (Cohen 1967: 642–43; cf., Strickon 1962; Goldstein 1971; and Pasternak 1972a, 1972b). A comparison of existing studies suggests that extended families (and especially joint families) may be particularly favored where the defense of accumulated wealth at one end of the socio-economic spectrum, or the maintenance of minimal standards of living at the other, are more efficiently ensured by retarding or suppressing family division, and that this is especially likely to be the situation in commercial-agricultural settings where essential productive resources are privately owned and are limited in supply constantly or periodically.

Many scholars assume that familial complexity declines in association with urbanization, commercialization, and industrialization. A difficulty arises since this impression is all too often based on a comparison between qualitatively different units. The adoption of a neolocal pattern of residence should not be confused with a propensity for conjugal or nuclear families. Many urban and rural studies that purport to deal with the "family" actually address themselves to "households" and, as a result, we often find ourselves comparing families in nonindustrialized societies with households in industrialized ones. As I observed earlier, the importance of the difference between households, which are essentially coresidential units and families, which are elementary corporate kinship units, must not be underestimated. The coincidence between household and family may be more likely in preindustrial than in industrial societies; the emergence of industrialization and urbanization might encourage families to adopt noncoresidential patterns and thereby to short-circuit natural fissiparous tendencies. If maintaining a common estate and an ability to shift resources effectively in a commercial setting does encourage the preservation of extended families, this may be even easier to accomplish if the constituent nuclear or stem units live separately and have infrequent contacts and few opportunities for intrafamilial confrontation. Failure to distinguish corporate kin groups from residential units in commercial settings may well obscure important or potentially important family relationships. In a study of East Indians in Uganda, for example, H. S. Morris (1959) proposed that a cash economy is not conducive to joint family operation because,

> wealth acquired by one member through his own efforts, which in traditional conditions is seldom an important category of property, can become of overriding significance. A man who has made a fortune by his own skill and who has invested it in property other than farming land may be reluctant to allow other members of the family to interfere in its management (1951: 781).

Morris' proposition is contradicted by Cohen's evidence that central-ized management of a multienterprise family investment can be so advan-tageous to the participating sub-units (households) that they may repress tendencies to family partition (Cohen 1967 and 1970). Furthermore, be-cause Morris does not distinguish between household and family he may actually have overlooked the presence of nonresidential joint families among the people he studied. His own data give rise to this suspicion; he says that, among the Indian families that he studied in Uganda, there were ninety households only ten of which were joint (Morris includes both stem and joint forms within this category). He also indicates that of these ten joint households only two were joint in the sense in which we have been using the term (i.e., consisting of two or more married sib-lings). But while Morris claims that Indians in Uganda do not realize the Indian extended family ideal, he observes:

> The surprising fact in the circumstances is that more households were not joint in this sense, which does not mean joint in the sense of sharing a common purse. On the other hand, of the ninety house-holds investigated, the heads of forty-four claimed to own property in India jointly with agnatic relations. To this extent the concept of a joint family as a property-owning corporation had some relevance, even in Uganda, where the form of the family was in fact almost always individual. Most informants, moreover, regretted this practi-cal disappearance of the joint family in East Africa, and attributed the loss to housing conditions, lack of proper religious training in the young, and European ideas which undermine control by the head of the household over sons and daughters-in-law (1959: 783).

It would be interesting to know whether Indian households in Uganda are sending or receiving anything to or from counterpart units in India (i.e., the other members of a "property-owning corporation"). What may have happened is that families in India may have subsidized far-flung ventures designed to ultimately increase total family resources and capa-bilities—a pattern also quite common among Chinese. And if an Indian household head in Uganda cannot maintain a subsistence does he have the right to return to, and to exert a claim upon, the family estate in India? Since Morris mentions no family partition there may well be such a residual right. If this is the case it is possible that, as I have suggested, the physical separation of family households may have actually postponed or even prevented family partition; it may have served to perpetuate the joint family, at least as a kind of insurance against failure. On the other hand, one could raise the question as to why Indian households *in Uganda* do not evolve into joint families. Crowded housing conditions might require the residential separation of family sub-units, but it would not prevent formation and perpetuation of nonresidential joint families. As for the impact of "new ideas on marriage," the question remains under what conditions are people more or less likely to adopt and conform to such ideas? When, for example, would a husband be most easily persuaded by a rebellious wife to leave his father's home? Perhaps he will be sympathetic to her entreaties only if there are no overriding economic reasons for resisting them. In this sense the quarreling of women in a joint family may be an indication of impending partition without actually being the cause. Morris produces other keys to the fragility of the family in Uganda. For one thing, property and inheritance laws interpose no obstacle to fission. Furthermore, Morris' description of family economics indicates how easy it is for a family to divide in Uganda (1959: 787–88). According to Morris,

> The migration and settlement of Indians in East Africa was by individuals and not by large blocks of patrilineal relatives, consequently a man in Uganda who wishes to rely on his lineage will be in difficulties. At the same time, in a trading community, men are in urgent need of support from friends and relatives. Capital and employment are often hard to come by and no one can afford to ignore any route that will lead him to successful help from a more powerful or rich man. No one can afford to ignore collateral or affinal links (1959: 788).

In short, survival of the East Indians in Uganda, as recent history has demonstrated, required them to rely upon each other. Cooperative mechanisms arose to unite Indians *as Indians* and it may have been partially for this reason that neither descent groups (patrilineages) nor extended families emerged in Uganda.

The ethnographic record certainly does not indicate that extended families as corporate entities are incompatible with urban-industrial or commercial settings (cf., Cohen 1967, 1970; Greenfield 1961-62; Strickon 1962; Johnson 1964; Rosen and Berlinck 1968; Pasternak 1972a, 1972b; and Clinget and Sween 1974). That married students live in cities away from the households of their parents does not mean that they constitute discrete corporate entities, or separate families. That a husband lives near the urban factory in which he is employed does not mean that his wife and children, back in the countryside, constitute a separate family. That a Chinese in southeast Asia has not seen his brother in years, has not sent money to him or received any from him, does not mean that he has renounced his claim upon the family estate. So long as a family estate in China has not been partitioned, brothers constitute a single family despite the national or international borders that may separate them. This family estate may provide family members with a kind of insurance they would not otherwise enjoy.

Although there are a number of industrial and commercial settings in which extended families (and even larger corporate kin groups) persist, some scholars would have us believe that these institutions persist only because the requirements of an industrial economy and society have not yet become fully operative (Goode 1963) or because no other agencies exist to provide economic and social security in a tight labor market marked by intense competitiveness and high unemployment (Ember 1967). But one could just as well argue that societies do not all provide these functions because they are, at least in some cases, already being adequately provided by various kinds of kinship groups. We must first determine the starting point for change—the kinds of kinship groups that exist in a society at the time commercialization and/or industrialization are introduced. We know that some societies, like many of those in western Europe, had nuclear family systems even *before* the development of industry so, even if industrialized societies do commonly encourage the nuclear family and neolocality, it may not be due to industrialization per se that these phenomena emerge. Some scholars have suggested that industrialization and commercialization do not necessarily isolate family units and individuals unless they are *already* isolated. There may be some process more general than either industrialization or commercialization that is responsible for the propensity for these forms.

Some scholars have proposed that female-focused families and households, like nuclear families and households, may be particularly common in commercial and/or industrial societies or may result from relationships with such societies. Peter Kunstadter (1963) suggested, for example, that:

> matrifocal families develop as a result of the division of labor separating adult males and adult females in a community; other solutions to problems of reproduction and residence in a community with an unbalanced adult sex ratio may be unavailable due to Western intervention, although these alternatives may not always be chosen when available (1963: 63).

In a similar vein Solien de Gonzáles proposed that

> the consanguineal household is an alternative type of domestic group which occurs in the process of acculturation of neoteric [i.e., modern]

societies in which the primary mechanism of Westernization is recurrent migratory labor with low remuneration (1965: 1547; cf., Otterbein 1965, 1970a).

Our understanding of the conditions that encourage female-focused families and households has been impeded by the familiar tendency to confuse households and families (cf., Otterbein 1965; Goode 1967; and Vicary 1967). Solien de Gonzáles pointed out that the distinctive feature of a "consanguineal" as opposed to an "affinal" household is the absence, in the former, of a husband-father (1965: 1541). He may not be present because his occupation requires him to live and work elsewhere, as is reportedly the case among some Caribbean peoples (see Solien 1960, 1965; cf., Otterbein 1965, 1970a), or perhaps because he is a professional soldier whose military obligations require constant or frequent mobility, as among the Nayar (Gough 1968). But the "matrifocal family," according to Solien, is something quite different:

> I would suggest that the term "matrifocality" be used to designate a type of family or household grouping in which the woman is dominant and plays the leading role psychologically (1965: 1544; cf., Smith 1956).

Matrifocal families and consanguineal households may coincide, but the correspondence is by no means inevitable. The family is matrifocal among the Mescalero Apache, for example, even though the husband-father is not absent (Boyer 1964). Among the Nayar, on the other hand, we find consanguineal households without matrifocal families since, as noted earlier, authority is vested in a woman's brother. The forces that remove a father-husband from the household of his wife and children do not necessarily remove him from their family. The conditions under which he is or is not likely to continue to be a member of their family remain unclear, and we have yet to determine with precision the conditions under which families or households are likely to be female-dominated or matrifocal.

The preceding discussion should make clear that if we hope to establish the conditions under which various forms of the family are likely to emerge in urban, commercial, or industrial contexts, or even to simply determine the frequency of various family forms in these settings, we will require more refined data—data that distinguishes sub-units of larger economic families from households.

8

The Principles
and Structures
of Descent

The term "descent" has been used in a variety of ways and has come to refer to a number of distinct things. The reader is undoubtedly already familiar with the biological meaning of descent, but descent can also have a jural meaning when it refers to a method of determining succession to property, social position, or rank (Radcliffe-Brown 1952: 32–49). Although the biological and jural meanings of descent usually coincide, the correspondence is by no means inevitable—heirs may be adopted or rejected, for example. When anthropologists employ the term "descent" they usually have the jural rather than the biological meaning of the term in mind.

Principles of Descent

Descent can be traced in a finite number of ways. "Unilineal descent" systems are those in which descent is consistently reckoned through relatives of the *same sex*. If an individual is assigned at birth to a group of kinsmen related to him exclusively through males the grouping that results is said to be based on "patrilineal" or "agnatic" descent (see Figure 8-1). If the individual is assigned at birth to a group of kinsmen related to him exclusively through females the group is based on "matrilineal" or "uterine" descent (see Figure 8-2). If we compare the two figures we see

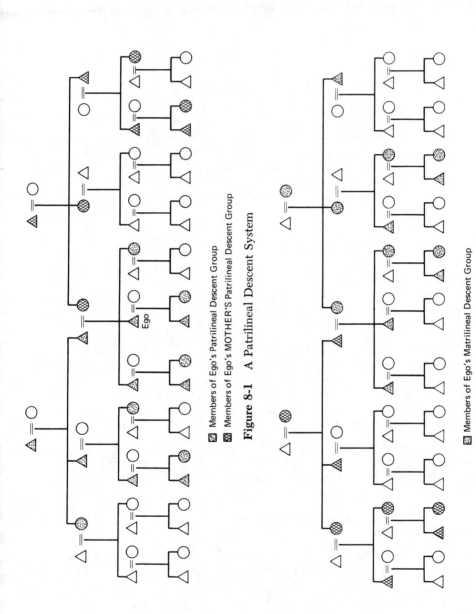

Figure 8-1 A Patrilineal Descent System

▨ Members of Ego's Patrilineal Descent Group

▩ Members of Ego's MOTHER'S Patrilineal Descent Group

Figure 8-2 A Matrilineal Descent System

▨ Members of Ego's Matrilineal Descent Group

▩ Members of Ego's FATHER'S Matrilineal Descent Group

Figure 8-3   A Parallel Descent System

that the relatives included in Ego's descent group differ depending on whether descent is traced patrilineally or matrilineally. We will see in Chapter 9 that which relatives are included can influence kinship nomenclature—the way in which Ego classifies his relatives and the terms he uses to refer to them. Patrilineal and matrilineal descent reckoning are the principles most commonly used to form descent groups in human society but descent can be handled in other ways. In some societies, for example, descent is traced both patrilineally and matrilineally. This is referred to as "double (unilineal)" descent. Ego is placed in the patrilineal descent group of his father for certain purposes but in the matrilineal descent group of his mother for others. Primary political and landholding units among the Yako of Eastern Nigeria are patrilineal descent groups, for example, but the same people also recognize matrilineal descent groups, units through which inheritance of moveable property takes place. In another method of unilineal descent reckoning, known as parallel descent, sons are supposedly placed in the descent group of their father and daughters in the group of their mother (see Figure 8-3). This procedure has been reported from Tibet (Goldstein 1971: 65) and has also been attributed to the Apinayé, a people of Brazil, although evidence for the practice in the case of the Apinayé has been seriously questioned (cf., Maybury-Lewis 1960 and Da Matta 1972).

Not all descent groups result from the consistent tracing of descent through relatives of the same sex; there are also many "nonunilineal," or "cognatic" descent groups found in the world. What they have in common is the fact that while descent determines group placement, it can be traced through *both* males and females (i.e., "ambilineally").

Cognatic Descent

Some anthropologists have expressed the belief that humans have a natural propensity for unilineal descent groups; a conviction supported by the simple fact that unilineal descent provides a basis for organization in most of the world's societies. Some scholars have even suggested that the absence of unilineal descent is not only rare but perhaps even abnormal (Radcliffe-Brown 1952: 48). Although most societies are uni-

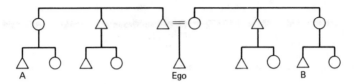

Figure 8-4   A Kindred

lineal, at least a third of them are not. Anthropologists have been taking a fresh look at nonunilineal, or cognatic kinship systems in recent years and we are becoming increasingly aware that humankind has invented a variety of them. A major breakthrough toward a better understanding of cognatic kinship was made when Ward Goodenough (1955) distinguished two kinds of cognatic groupings that had previously been lumped together —the "kindred" and the "nonunilineal descent group." A kindred is a group of individuals all of whom have a relative in common. A single Ego constitutes the group referent and all relationships are traced to him through either males or females. As Davenport has pointed out, "each person has his own kindred, the personnel and boundaries of which coincide only with those of his siblings, and siblings are members of as many different kindreds as there are kin types" (1959: 562). All members of a kindred are considered related to the referent Ego, but not necessarily to each other as Figure 8-4 indicates. All first cousins of Ego in Figure 8-4 are members of his kindred, but /A/ is not considered a member of the kindred of /B/ since they are not first cousins with respect to each other. In other words, a kindred is defined *laterally* or, more properly, "bilaterally" from a referent individual and those included may be specified in terms of the degree of their relationship traced laterally from that individual. A kindred is therefore in no sense a *descent* group. Since no two individuals (with the exception of siblings) have identical kindreds, many people have supposed that a kindred cannot be corporate—that it cannot preserve continuity of possession of some property or estate. How could a kindred maintain continuity of anything if its composition changes with each referent! While it is generally true that kindreds are not corporate, there are exceptions. As Davenport pointed out,

> a personal kindred can become a landowning and landholding group with continuity, just like a descent group, if the title to the land is vested in a single individual with the limitation that it must be distributed and redistributed among his personal kindred and cannot be alienated without their consent (1959: 564).

It is thus possible that members of a kindred who do not themselves have title to a piece of kindred land can nevertheless claim some of it to use or can exert some influence over its disposition. So long as there is some kind of patterned rule of succession like "primogeniture" (i.e., inheritance by first child), the corporation will have continuity even though the particular members of the kindred change with each succession and change of kindred focus. Kindreds of this sort are found among the Ifugao and Kalinga of the Philippines, where a system of primogeniture keeps land intact.

The formation of kindreds always involves some degree of collateral limitation on the extension of kinship statuses or positions (Davenport refers to this as collateral restriction). Societies differ in this regard—in some cases maternal and paternal second cousins are members of the kindred, for example, while third cousins are not. In other cases fourth cousins are included, etc. We have yet to discover the factors that determine different degrees of collateral restriction. In some instances there is an unequal restriction on the paternal and maternal sides and groups of this sort are sometimes referred to as "skewed" kindreds. A case in point would be the Chinese *Wu Fu,* or "Mourning Grades." When an individual dies relatives on the maternal and paternal sides mourn him. Mourning obligations (e.g., length of mourning period, type of mourning garments to be worn, etc.) differ according to the precise relationship one has with the deceased but, generally speaking, obligations are heavier on the paternal than on the maternal side and are extended to more individuals. This skewing of mourning obligations is undoubtedly related to the general patrilineal emphasis that is characteristic of Chinese society (see Wolf 1970b).

A "nonunilinear" kin group is a cognatic group quite different from a kindred. Davenport called this group a "Sept," Firth referred to it as a "ramage," and still others have spoken of "ambilineal" descent groups. What these terms have in common is the fact that they refer to a group of people all of whom acknowledge *descent* from a common ancestor. What makes them different from unilineal descent groups is the fact that descent can be traced *either* or sometimes through *both* males and females —it is not unilineally traced. In contrast to kindreds, on the other hand, ambilineal descent groups include individuals with an *ancestor* in common rather than with a living relative in common. Because the group referent or focus does not change with each generation, membership boundaries are also fixed. Again in contrast to kindreds all members of a nonunilineal descent group, being descendants of a common ancestor, are related to each other (see Figure 8-5).

There is another rare form of descent reckoning which produces a

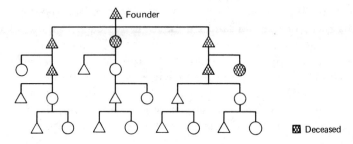

Figure 8-5   An Ambilineal Descent Group

group that some anthropologists refer to as a "rope." The principle upon which such groups are constructed involves a regular and consistent mixing of patrilineal and matrilineal links. In brief, a rope is a descent group made up of cross-sex, parent-child relationships (see Figure 8-6). Such descent reckoning has been reported among the Mundugamor and Banaro of New Guinea (see Mead 1968).

Unilineal Descent

Although the principles by which descent can be reckoned are numerous, it is most commonly traced unilineally—through relatives of the same sex. It is generally assumed that a unilocal rule of residence is a necessary precondition for the development of unilineal descent. As we have seen, a unilocal rule of residence has the effect of aggregating relatives of a particular sort. A patrilocal rule aggregates males related through males, a matrilocal rule aggregates females related through females, and an avunculocal rule of residence aggregates males related through females (see pages 44–45). Thus, if a people consistently observe a patrilocal rule of residence and *if* they have descent groups, then in all probability they will have patrilineal descent groups. If people adopt a matrilocal or avunculocal rule of residence and have descent groups, then they will probably be matrilineal groups. The primary question, of course, is under which conditions are people more or less likely to have descent groups of any sort. Although the adoption of a particular residence rule may

Figure 8-6   A Rope

influence the kind of descent group people form, it will not account for the emergence of such groups. The fact that unilocal residence spatially aggregates people descended from a common ancestor does not mean that they will either characterize themselves as a descent group or that they will organize and function as a group. There are many societies that have a unilocal rule of residence but lack unilineal descent groups. Elman Service has speculated that the notion of descent may have first emerged in tribal society as a mechanism for linking local groups into larger alliances (1962). The implication is that in paleolithic times, hunting-gathering bands did not generally have descent groups. We will have more to say about this speculation shortly.

Cross-cultural support is available for the assertion that unilocality is a necessary but not sufficient condition for the presence of unilineal descent groups. A recent study (Ember, Ember & Pasternak, 1974) revealed that while a majority of societies with unilineal descent (i.e., about 97 percent of the selected sample, or 350 of 360 societies) also have a unilocal rule of residence, unilocality is not invariably associated with unilineal descent; only 72 percent (or 350 out of 485 societies) of the sample's unilocal societies also had unilineal descent groups. In other words, unilineal societies are usually also unilocal, but not all unilocal societies are unilineal; rule of residence may influence rule of descent but it probably is not a sufficient cause of unilineal descent reckoning.

Some anthropologists have speculated that it was a strong notion of private property together with a unilocal rule of residence that favored development of unilineal descent groups (Lowie 1961 and Murdock 1949). Property presupposes mechanisms for clearly defining rights and descent grouping provides an effective-way to accomplish this since it results in units with continuing and clearcut membership. But property rights are likely to have developed in human history when access to productive resources became problematic—that is, when there arose a threat that others might claim rights to scarce things that people needed to survive. Elman Service speculated that descent reckoning may have first emerged in human history as a device for linking local groups in the face of competition, and recent cross-cultural evidence provides some indirect support for this speculation. If warfare, an obvious indicator of competition, is introduced as a consideration we can greatly improve our ability to predict the presence of unilineal descent. In one sample of societies, 94 percent of the cases with unilineal descent were also characterized by fighting between communities or larger territorial groups and a unilocal rule of residence (Ember, Ember & Pasternak, 1974). In other words, descent grouping is associated with, and is predicted by, unilocal residence *and* intergroup fighting. It is probable that, where intergroup fighting is likely, natural selection favors customs and institutions that provide affiliation

with clearly defined groups of people who can be relied upon in time of
need. In societies with a high level of political development such affiliation may be provided by membership in a centralized political unit;
e.g., we call upon the state for our defense. But where political development is not so advanced, unilineal descent may constitute an especially
fitting response to the challenge of competing groups (cf., Sahlins 1961).

There is some evidence that age-classes or warrior societies may constitute additional solutions, especially in societies characterized by high
mobility and low population density (e.g., among some Plains Indians and
East African nomadic pastoralists). In some societies people are organized
into classes consisting of individuals of the same sex who fall within cul-
turally defined age ranges. Members of the same age-class move through
crucial life stages together. The Jie pastoralists discussed earlier in connection with family organization have such an organization, for example,
as do most Nilotic peoples (Gulliver 1968: 338–40). Jie males are ascribed
to ordered generations, the most important of which are the senior or
initiated generation and the junior or uninitiated one. Every twenty-five
years special rituals mark the establishment of a new generation of Jie.
Once begun, initiations for a particular generation are held about once
every three years and individuals initiated during the same year belong
to the same age-group. Three consecutive age-groups constitute an age-
set within a given generation. Gulliver describes the functions of this
age-class organization as follows:

> Although the age group and seniority system is only marginally
> concerned with the nonritual aspects of Jie public life, it is the only
> large-scale organization they have. Settlements are united into func-
> tioning districts, and these again into the whole tribe, principally by
> ritual requirements and through the mechanism of the age group
> system. . . . Both district and tribe are significantly defined in
> ritual terms, but the unity obtained in this way spreads over into
> nonritual matters to give a general cohesion to the society (Gulliver
> 1968: 340).

In some societies age-class organization provides the nexus of political
authority. Such is the case among the Karimojong of Uganda, where members of the active senior generation perform administrative, judicial, and
religious functions while members of the junior generation are warriors
and policemen. Noninitiates and members of the retired generation are
essentially without function (Dyson-Hudson 1966). Among the Nyakyusa
of southeastern Africa, the members of a particular age-set even live apart
in age-villages (Wilson: 1963).

The Cheyenne Indians of the American Plains provide an example of
organization in terms of warrior societies. The Cheyenne had some five

named military associations, each of which was open to male candidates (of any age) who could demonstrate physical fitness for warfare. A man usually sought entry into the warrior society of his father. Each of these associations had its own costumes, dances, and songs, and their leaders comprised the most important war chiefs of the tribe. Cheyenne warrior associations constituted the tribe's military and police force (Hoebel 1960).

Sodalities of these sorts, like guilds, unions, and lodges, make it possible to solicit support from a larger number of individuals than would be possible if one had to rely only upon those unilineal kinsmen that happened to be nearby and available at a given moment. As Elman Service suggested,

> when seasonal and yearly fluctuations in food resources prevent the formation of cohesive residential groups, it is more likely that the social organization itself will become more complex-seeming and more formal as sodalities and associated statuses come about to make possible cooperation in military, economic, and ceremonial affairs (1962: 75).

Another anthropologist, Robert Anderson, has expressed the belief that cross-kin associations may be relatively recent additions to the human cultural inventory. He holds a somewhat different view of the circumstances under which they may have emerged, however. According to Anderson,

> The history of formal common interest associations during the first million years or so of human existence lends itself to brief statement: there were virtually none. We can say this with confidence, even though the evidence is what a court of law would term circumstantial. Because they normally lived in small bands scattered thinly across forests and plains, paleolithic and mesolithic men would not normally have formed groups on the basis of common interest rather than of territory or kinship. Their needs could have been totally met as societies of small bands of related families roving circumscribed territories (1971: 209).

Anderson suggests that the earliest cross-kin sodalities probably "flickered into life" no earlier than 25,000 B.C. when, according to his interpretation of archaeological evidence, some kind of religious activity first seems to have appeared in human society. It is Anderson's belief that the earliest common-interest associations probably served to unite individuals in terms of religious beliefs (1971: 209–10). Where contemporary nomadic hunter-gatherers have such sodalities, in his view, it may well be that they have borrowed them from more advanced peoples. Their presence among nomadic hunter-gatherers could also reflect a process of devolution from a tribal level of societal integration (cf., Martin 1969), although Anderson does not mention this possibility. In any event, Anderson's position is that the emergence of cross-kin sodalities was probably associated less with mobile populations than with relatively sedentary communities (villages), which were themselves made possible in most cases by the discovery of cultivation. Anderson suggests that it was during the period of human history when neolithic villages were not yet integrated into complex political and economic systems that the elaboration of cross-kin sodalities was probably most encouraged (1971: 210). This part of Anderson's speculation roughly parallels Service's proposal that sodalities *in general* proliferated in tribal society. Furthermore, according to Anderson,

> even though voluntary associations were prominent in the neolithic, and even though they have become prominent in recent, postindustrial societies, they were often restricted or absent in major parts of stratified, urban societies of the preindustrial sort. Put differently, between the crests of association development in neolithic communities and modern industrial nations lies a trough of quiescence, when the importance of associations was comparatively reduced (1971: 213).

The reason for the "quiescence" of cross-kin sodalities in preindustrialized, stratified, urban contexts according to Anderson may have been that the emerging state, in most instances, usurped most of their functions (1971: 214). With the development of urban-industrial society, however, there emerged a new need for institutions "on an intermediate level, larger than the family, yet smaller than the state" (1971: 215), and a new proliferation of cross-kin associations was begun.

A recent cross-cultural study by M. L. Ritter (1974) provides some empirical support for these speculations concerning the late emergence of cross-kin sodalities. Ritter's study provides particular support for Service's speculation since it reveals a statistically significant association between strength of age-class systems, frequency of warfare, and fluctuating size and composition of local groups. Her study further indicated that age-class systems comprise integrating mechanisms *additional* to, rather than alternative to, descent groups.

Ambilineal descent may also provide unambiguous manpower for offense or defense so long as membership in groups formed on this basis is not overlapping. But ambilineal descent is probably produced, at least in part, by bilocal or multilocal residence and, as noted earlier, there is reason to believe that multilocal residence is most often the result of recent depopulation. If this is so, then ambilineal descent may, for the most part, be an even more recent invention in the history of humankind.

Descent and Societal Complexity

Some anthropologists have observed that unilineal descent principles provide a basis for grouping people in societies of all levels of cultural development and complexity and in all major geographic areas of the world. G. P. Murdock noted, for example, that,

> among the most primitive or culturally undeveloped tribes . . . the Andamanese pygmies, the Paiute of the Great Basin, and the Yahgan of Tiera del Fuego are bilateral in descent, the Vedda of Ceylon, the Rankokamekra of east-central Brazil, and the Kutchin of northern Canada are matrilineal, and the Witoto of Amazonia, the Gilyak of Siberia, and the Miwok of California are patrilineal, while several native Australian tribes are characterized by double descent. All rules of descent are likewise well represented on the intermediate levels of culture, among agricultural and developed pastoral people. Even among the literate peoples with relatively complex civilizations, our sample includes the bilateral Yankees and Syrian Christians, the patrilineal Chinese and Manchus and the matrilineal Minangkabau Malays of Sumatra and Brahman Nayars of India (1949: 186).

Murdock implies that since all rules of descent are represented in societies of all degrees of complexity there is no association between descent and societal complexity. His conviction was based on a comparison of contemporary or near contemporary societies, however, and just because we find descent groups among contemporary hunters and gatherers we cannot assume that their paleolithic forebears also had them. It could be, as Elman Service speculated, that the idea of descent emerged later in human cultural development (1962: 116–18). But even on the basis of contemporary populations Murdock's statement presents problems. When David Aberle (1961) compared 564 societies in terms of subsistence technique and principle of descent, he discovered that while all rules of descent were found in association with all subsistence settings they were not found with equal frequency in all contexts (see Table 8-1). A majority of ethnographically described hunting-gathering peoples (60 percent) are bilateral. Although not all bilateral societies are hunter-gatherers, and while not all hunter-gatherers are bilateral, people at this level of technological sophistication are significantly more likely to be bilateral than are people at any other level. This is not really surprising considering the advantages that such people may derive from flexible group membership. We recall that bilocality was significantly more common in societies with

Table 8-1   DESCENT AND TYPES OF SUBSISTENCE*

Subsistence Type	Descent System									
	Patrilineal		Bilateral		Matrilineal		Duolineal		Total	
	No.	(%)	No.	(%)	No.	(%)	No.	(%)	No.	(%)
Plow agriculture	69	(59)	38	(32)	9	(8)	1	(1)	117	(100)
Horticulture	109	(41)	86	(32)	57	(21)	15	(6)	267	(100)
Pastoralism	51	(65)	19	(24)	5	(6)	4	(5)	79	(100)
Extractive (Hunting & Gathering)	19	(19)	61	(60)	13	(13)	8	(8)	101	(100)
Totals	248	(44)	204	(36)	84	(15)	28	(5)	564	(100)

* Source: Summary of table in Aberle 1961: 677.

a mean community size under ninety-nine than over ninety-nine, and bilaterality is particularly appropriate to such a residence pattern. Where subsistence is provided by horticulture or plow agriculture we usually find some form of unilineal descent (i.e., patrilineal, matrilineal, or double descent). Although matrilineal descent reckoning is not especially common at any level of technological development, if we find it at all it is significantly more likely to be found in association with some form of horticulture than in any other technological context. While not all pastoral peoples are patrilineal, the figures in Table 8-1 indicate that pastoral societies are significantly more likely to reckon descent patrilineally than are people employing any other technology. Aberle suggests that the overwhelming patrilineality of pastoral peoples may relate to a particularly intimate relationship between this form of subsistence and cooperation among males. Patrilineality is also the major principle of descent among people with plow cultivation although bilaterality seems rather well represented in such settings as well. In brief, then, although we cannot predict the rule of descent a people will employ simply on the basis of the nature of their technology, it is clear that some rules of descent are significantly more likely to occur in certain technological contexts than in others.

Allan Coult and Robert Habenstein (1965: 524) tabulated the relationship between unilineal descent and level of political integration (see Table 8-2). Their figures indicate that while societies at all levels of political development are more likely to employ a unilineal principle of descent than not, societies that are mid-range in terms of political complexity (i.e., Peace Groups, Minimal and Small States in Table 8-2) are significantly more likely to be unilineal than societies that are politically simpler

Table 8-2   UNILINEAL DESCENT AND LEVEL OF POLITICAL INTEGRATION*

Level of Political Integration	Number of Societies (Totals)	Number Unilineal	Percent Unilineal†
No Local Level Integration	35	19	(54)
Politically Independent Local Groups Not Over 1500 in Average Population	225	132	(59)
Peace Groups Transcending the Local Community, but Where the Basis of Unity Is Not Political	18	12	(67)
Minimal States—Politically Integrated Units Averaging Between 1500 and 10,000	118	90	(76)
Small States—Politically Integrated Units Averaging Between 10,000 and 100,000	52	44	(85)
States—Politically Integrated Units Averaging at Least 100,000	78	42	(54)
Totals	526	339	(64)

* Source: Coult and Habenstein 1965.
† That is Patrilineal, Matrilineal, or Double Descent.

or more complex. Although the figures suggest a particular harmony between societies of mid-range political complexity and descent grouping they do not indicate an incompatibility between descent grouping and either very simple or very complex political integration.

It is not enough to talk only of unilineal descent principles and the conditions under which they will occur; we must also consider the structures through which various principles or rules are manifested and expressed. There are many kinds of patrilineal and matrilineal descent groups. Some are associated with certain economic and political conditions while others are not. It is true that the Tungus, Tiv, and Chinese all use a patrilineal principle to organize descent groups, but the *kinds* of groups formed are radically different in each case and the differences probably reflect the social, economic, and political contexts in which each people live, a point made some years ago by Morton Fried (1957). As Fried noted, some descent groups are corporate in that they maintain continuity of possession to an estate of some sort, while others are not. Not all descent groups own things. The Chinese believe that people with the same surname share a common patrilineal ancestor somewhere in the past and should not marry. At this level the only function of descent is to regulate marriage. But, as we shall presently see, the Chinese also form *corporate* descent groups which include only some individuals of a given surname.

Descent groups may also be distinguished in terms of whether descent is "demonstrated" or only "stipulated." By stipulated we mean that common descent is simply assumed—there is no concerted effort to specify the precise connections between an ancestor's various descendants. Where descent is demonstrated precise linkages become important and people may even maintain written records, or genealogies, to keep track of their connections. When descent groups are predicated on stipulated descent they are commonly referred to as clans or sibs, and where descent is demonstrated they are usually termed lineages. If descent is merely stipulated, the effect is to *include* as many people as possible rather than to highlight distinctions within the descent group. The demonstration of descent allows the progeny of an ancestor to discriminate among themselves for one purpose or another. Members of a descent group might want to distinguish degrees of access to group resources—to privileges, ranks, or properties—or to define degrees of mutual obligation and responsibility.

Descent groups may also be contrasted in terms of whether they are egalitarian, ranked, or stratified. Ranking has to do with positions of relative *prestige* and is not necessarily associated with differences in wealth or in terms of access to strategic resources. As Fried defined it,

> ranking exists when the following conditions are simultaneously present: (a) there is a social limitation of the number of positions of high prestige, so that at any given time it is probable that there are more qualified persons than positions; (b) the principles upon which statuses of high prestige are assigned to individuals are based upon criteria other than sex, age, and ephemeral personal attributes, though these criteria generally continue to operate in a supplementary way; (c) the resultant hierarchy of statuses is objective, i.e., different individuals in the same group do not have discrete conceptions of the hierarchy or the identity of the persons who fill the statuses. Rank by this definition has a variable relation to wealth and the control of access to strategic resources (1957: 23–24).

Where adult members of the same sex in a group enjoy different rights of access to strategic resources, to the things necessary for production and for subsistence, then we are dealing not simply with ranking but with stratification (Fried 1957: 24). In the case of Chinese rice cultivators strategic resources might include such items as land, labor, water, and capital.

Let us now compare the descent groups of three peoples in the light of these distinctions—those of the reindeer-herding Tungus of Siberia, the shifting-agricultural Tiv of Nigeria, and the sedentary-agricultural Chinese.

The exogamous, egalitarian clans of the Tungus provide members with rights in territory and reindeer; they protect members and enforce various social rules. Reflecting the fundamentally egalitarian nature of Tungus society, no distinctions are made among clan members; all are considered equally descended from the common ancestor. Tiv society is also strongly egalitarian—there is even some resistance to unusual displays of authority (see Bohannan 1958). There are neither legislators nor enforcers—only men of relative influence. Members of the Tiv patrilineage share territorial and ceremonial rights and have common political obligations in feuding and warfare (Bohannan 1954). Because it cross-cuts local settlements, the lineage performs an important integrating political function. Although Tiv society, like that of the Tungus, is basically egalitarian, distinctions are made within the descent group and considerable attention is given to genealogy. The Tiv patrilineage is organized in terms of a principle that some anthropologists have referred to as the "principle of segmentary opposition":

> The principle, in agnatic groups, is an extremely simple one. It is a projection of the idea that my brother and I are antagonistic to each other only so long as there is no person more distantly related to us who is antagonistic to both of us. I join my brother against my half brothers. My half brothers join me and my full brothers against the group of our father's brother's sons. They join us, again, against our father's father's brother's son's sons (Bohannan 1963: 137).

In Figure 8-7 below, /a/ and /b/ represent discrete agnatic groups descended from a common ancestor (i.e., from /1/). When it comes to political action and support, and especially where feuding erupts, agnatic group /a/ will stand against group /b/ unless someone from group /c/ makes trouble, in which case /a/ and /b/ unite as a single group (/1/) to fight group /2/. Should an altercation involve a member of group /h/, there would be an opposition between agnatic segments /A/ and /B/.

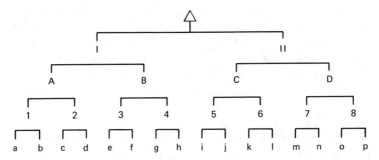

Figure 8-7 The Principle of Segmentary Opposition

Should someone from /m/ become involved in a feud with a member of /a/, the confrontation could involve segments /I/ and /II/, and an attack perpetrated by an outsider would unite the entire descent group.

Despite its segmentary nature, the Tiv lineage, like the Tungus clan, is egalitarian—reflecting the nature of Tiv society itself. All members of the descent group are equally descended from the founding ancestor and are equally members of the descent group. Segments at any level are also equivalent—/I/ and /II/ are units of essentially the same sort as are segments /A/, /B/, /C/, and /D/ or /1/, /2/, /3/, etc. The descent group is segmented symmetrically in the sense that there is a balancing of units in each generation—segments are always posed against similar segments. An ancestor without a brother cannot constitute the focus of a lineage segment since there can be no opposite. The Tiv lineage is integrated, to use Durkheim's term, "mechanically"—in terms of units essentially of the same sort. But lineages may also be integrated "organically" —on the basis of different, specialized parts. Such groups are particularly characteristic of societies that are either ranked only or both ranked and stratified.

Some years ago Paul Kirchhoff (1968) distinguished two kinds of descent groups—an equalitarian and a conical type. Conical structures are organically integrated and are especially suited to ranked societies, where they are frequently found. We find them among the Nootka, the Tahitians, the Trobriand Islanders, and the Kalinga, for example. Kirchhoff noted that the most distinctive features of conical descent groups are that they are ranked and that they lack exclusive or invariable exogamy. Although they may be patrilineal or matrilineal in principle, ambilineality is often allowed or tolerated, especially for certain segments of the descent group. As we shall see, the absence of strict exogamy and the presence of de facto ambilineality are both closely related to the ranked nature of the societies in which such descent groups are found.

Conical descent groups usually focus on a specific item of property, moveable or immoveable—like land, rank, or privilege of some sort. Within the descent group a dominant line of descent (which Kirchhoff called the "aristoi") enjoys special privileges with respect to this property and the kinds of privileges enjoyed by people in collateral lines of descent depends on their genealogical distance from the main line. In other words, the system is one of fundamental inequality in terms of status and privilege.

Imagine a society in which privilege and prestige are concentrated consistently in the line of first children (i.e., a system of primogeniture). The line of first children constitutes what Kirchhoff called the "aristoi," and development of the descent group involves a continuous sloughing off of collateral lines, each of which has different rights and privileges

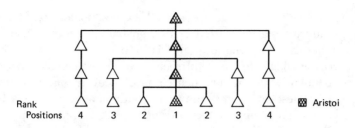

Rank
Positions   4   3   2   1   2   3   4   ▨ Aristoi

Figure 8-8   A Conical Descent Group

(see Figure 8-8). Nearness of relationship to the common ancestor thus becomes an important determinant of status and privilege and, for this reason, precise genealogical linkages must be remembered. Parallel cousin marriage and ambilineal descent reckoning are likely in the case of individuals with relatively high rank position because both provide a way to acquire maximal rank position and privilege. By marrying his patrilateral parallel cousin, Ego in Figure 8-9 makes it possible for his son to trace descent (through his mother) to the line of aristoi and thereby to acquire greater privilege and status than if he had married a woman of inferior genealogical position.

A conical descent group is clearly hierarchical and in this sense differs from either the egalitarian clans of the Tungus or the egalitarian lineage of the Tiv. It is integrated organically rather than mechanically because lines of descent differ in terms of privileges and status. In contrast to the Tiv case the process of segmentation is asymmetrical, resulting in units that do not balance each other. As we shall see, the conical descent group is not the only kind of asymmetrically segmented lineage that humans have invented. Where stratification has emerged, and where rights of access to strategic resources have come to be obtained in nongenealogical ways (i.e., not exclusively through inheritance), we may find yet another kind of organically integrated descent group. We will describe such a group shortly.

On the basis of a study of social stratification in Polynesia, Marshall

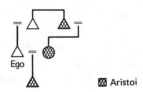

Ego

▨ Aristoi

Figure 8-9   The Consequence of Descent Group Endogamy,
Parallel Cousin Marriage, and Ambilineality
in a Conical Descent Group

Sahlins (1958) suggested that we should expect nonlocalized, conical descent groups to replace localized, egalitarian ones under certain environmental conditions. If a given local area is supplied with most or with all the resources available to the total society, each settlement can coexist fairly independently and, under such circumstances, we might expect to find egalitarian descent groups. But if a locality cannot provide a broad resource base, it must employ ties with other settlements to supplement locally available resources. Items needed may be obtained through simple trade or by means of customary payments. Exchange between coastal and inland villages in Trobriands was of this sort—fish for garden produce, protein for carbohydrates. If a whole island lacks an important resource, trade may have to be even more complex. In the Trobriand *Kula* trade a chief functioned as an entrepreneur; he organized the construction of seagoing canoes and the conduct of interisland trade. But let us now suppose that there is an uneven distribution of resources on a given island and that a growing population begins to compete for them. Short of warfare (which was in fact common on many Polynesian islands) one might expect the development of discrimination in terms of rights and privileges, with distinctions possibly being made in terms of such social devices as primogeniture. It is under such circumstances that conical descent groups might be expected to emerge.

In an attempt to control an even wider resource base a localized conical descent group might settle branches in areas with access to resources not available to the main branch, and a nonlocalized conical descent group could evolve. Large parts of an island might be occupied by a single conical descent group, the segments of which are regarded as being strongly linked genealogically. According to Sahlins, the emergence of nonlocalized conical descent groups may signal an important step in the direction of true stratification and the state. In time, one descent group may dominate the others; it may even succeed in controlling chiefly statuses throughout an island or area by replacing the heads of other descent groups with their own appointees. Such a process seems to have taken place in Tahiti, Hawaii, and in some African states.

As indicated in chapter 7, many scholars have questioned the degree to which kin groups in general, and descent groups in particular, can tolerate social and economic differentiation and still remain viable and effective. Kirchhoff observed, for example, that when the interests of the aristoi as a group become contradictory with those of the descent group as a whole, the descent group is replaced by distinctions of class:

> The process of differentiation within the clan, while for a long time taking place within this flexible unit, finally reaches the point where the interests of those of equal standing, in *all* the clans of the

tribe, come into such sharp conflicts with the interests of the other strata that their struggles, the struggle of by now fully-fledged social classes, overshadows the old principles of clanship and finally leads to the break-up of clan, first as the dominating form of social organization and then to its final disappearance (1968: 379–380).

Others have made much the same point. Paul Bohannan suggested, for example, that "if unilineal descent groups are found, they are found for the most part in societies of medium size that have fairly adequate means of exploitation of their environments" (1963: 136); and Meyer Fortes wrote, "it seems that corporate descent groups can exist only in more or less homogeneous societies" (1953: 26). The common impression here is that descent grouping and stratification are incompatible or at least antagonistic phenomena, and some have suggested that descent grouping and strong, centralized states are also antagonistic. Frederick Engles suggested that there is an "irreconcilable opposition" between the existence of descent groups in general and the presence of state organization. According to Engels, the emergence of the latter ultimately produces an erosion of the former:

> The first attempt at forming a state consists in breaking up the gentes [or clans] by dividing their members into those with privileges and those with none, and by further separating the latter into two productive classes and thus setting them one against the other (1942: 99).

And Yehudi Cohen pointed out that:

> Part of the course of a state's vertical entrenchment is the arrogation by its leaders of the exclusive right to wage war, enact and administer laws, control productivity and redistribute wealth, lay claim to rights of eminent domain and administer tenure, exact tribute, and the like. These are among the rights that are also claimed by the controlling personnel of corporate kin groups and communities. Since such authority and other political activities can be carried out autonomously in only one of the two boundary systems, one of them must be subverted if the society is to remain stable (1969: 665–666).

Inherent in such statements is the conviction that when differential access to strategic resources emerges in society, and when it becomes possible to accumulate wealth independently (e.g., from trade or industry), the descent group, even where it is ranked, ceases to reflect economic and political reality. Those with special access to the means of production and its fruits come to have more in common with each other than with less fortunate members of their respective descent groups. Imagine what would happen in a conical descent group if an individual of low rank struck it rich while his "aristoi" cousin remained relatively poor. A serious contradiction would emerge if a genealogical nobody ended up a controller of strategic resources and a purveyor of political and economic influence.

It is undoubtedly true that the development of stratification and the emergence of the state encouraged mechanisms capable of integrating society across and independent of kinship lines. But, as Fried (1957) pointed out, the development of supra-kin organization in society does not mean that there is a fundamental incompatibility between descent groups per se and either stratification or state organization; some descent groups are quite capable of accommodating both phenomena. For purposes of illustration consider a kind of descent group that, until recently, was common in southeastern China (see Freedman 1958; 1966). All members of a Chinese lineage are equally descended from a common, founding ancestor. The Chinese lineage shares this feature with the Tiv and Tungus descent groups. The important difference between the Tiv lineage (a conical descent group) and a Chinese lineage is that segments of the latter are not genealogically determined but rather reflect socioeconomic position in society at large. Let us see how this works:

Chinese traditionally recognize two kinds of property—private property, which can be freely acquired, lent, rented, or sold by an individual; and ancestral property which, once established, cannot be divided, alienated, or disposed of without the consent of all shareholders. Any man of means may set aside a portion of his private property to establish an ancestral estate, the profits of which will be used to underwrite periodic sacrifices to his ghost after he has passed away. A portion of the estate's profits may also be used to finance the education of gifted descendants or for the welfare of poor progeny. Private property is equally divided among a man's sons when he dies, but an ancestral trust becomes the corporate property of his descendants.

In order for a lineage segment to come into being, a focal ancestor must be designated and an ancestral estate or trust must be established in his name. It is not always the focal ancestor himself who is responsible for an ancestral trust; in many cases estates are posthumously established by sons, grandsons, or even later progeny. That these relatives select him and not some other ancestor as a focus for their corporate trust is no accident. The establishment of any ancestral estate (and lineage segment) requires an accumulation and concentration of wealth among certain members of the descent group. Since, as group membership grows, some descendants do well while others become impoverished, wealth and status may come to be distributed unevenly within the group. Reflecting the stratified nature of society as a whole, only certain members of the descent group

have the wherewithal to set land aside as an ancestral trust. When sufficient wealth has been accumulated in one branch or line of the descent
group, and when it is decided that an ancestral trust should be established, an attempt is made to ensure that earnings will not be drained,
diluted, or consumed by distant agnates. The more shareholders in an
ancestral estate the less profit available per share. For this reason, those
who establish an ancestral trust usually prefer more immediate focal
ancestors to more distant ones.

What should be especially noted about the Chinese lineage portrayed
in Figure 8-10 is that, unlike the Tiv lineage, segments are not invariably
balanced by equivalent units. The descendants of ancestor /B2/ function
as a lineage segment or branch—they attend common feasts and ceremonies, they enjoy in common the profits of ancestral trust /B2/, etc.
They constitute a lineage within a larger lineage. The same is true of the

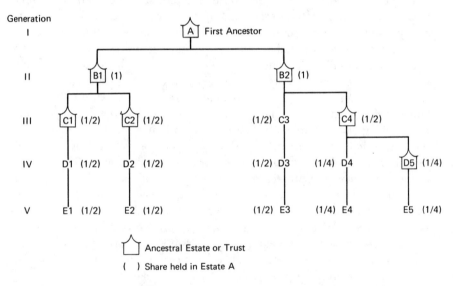

Figure 8-10   Segmentation in a Chinese Lineage

descendants of /C4/. But the progeny of /C3/, for whom no ancestral
estate has been established, do not constitute a counterpart segment to
/C4/ because they lack a corporate focus. Also, /C4/ and /D5/ are without
counterparts. The fact that /E5/ has access to more ancestral trusts than
any other agnate in his generation (only he has access to estates /D5/,
/C4/, /B2/, and /A/) suggests that his ancestors were probably unusually
favored in terms of the accumulation of wealth. One might also predict
that his ancestors have had a major voice in lineage affairs, that they

provided the best educated and most politically influential members of the group.

In theory, headship in Chinese lineage or lineage branch was passed by age and generation rather than by seniority of descent line—there were no aristoi here. The lineage head was supposedly the oldest living member of the senior generation in the descent group. Theoretically, then, the Chinese lineage was egalitarian since anyone who lives long enough could become a headman. But in reality leadership and responsibility for management was concentrated in the hands of the wealthy and literate. Thus both the pattern of segmentation and the nature of leadership manifest the basic inegalitarian and stratified nature of Chinese society.

It is true that when the Chinese state was strong, the descent group tended to be relatively weak and when the state was weak, the descent group became stronger and sometimes even managed to usurp some of the functions and powers of the state. Despite such fluctuations in relative power, however, the descent group has shown itself to be extraordinarily viable and tenacious in China. What accounts for the viability of the Chinese lineage in the face of so strong and centralized a polity? How could so internally differentiated a descent group have survived? Far from being weakened by its heterogeneity, the Chinese lineage seems to have been strengthened by it. So long as real power within the group was concentrated in the hands of an elite, and so long as the importance of genealogical authority and states were minimized, the lineage could effectively hold its members together. It could fortify them against their neighbors and soften the demands and exactions of the state. The wealthy and literate provided protection (political and economic). The poor could rent lands owned by lineage branches and, in some cases, could obtain support for the education of particularly gifted children or funds in time of dire need, all from the profits of ancestral trusts and estates. From the point of view of the wealthy, membership and participation by poor agnates in the descent group was useful since they constituted the armed force necessary for the protection of their own class interests.

Although the Chinese political system was highly centralized, it allowed a great measure of autonomy to local communities which, especially in southeastern China, often meant to local descent groups. From the point of view of the central government this was a more efficient method of ensuring stability and control in the countryside—it was certainly cheaper than stationing soldiers in every remote part of the country. The strong centralized state was no fiction in China, but neither was the strong descent group. They were by no means antagonistic or mutually exclusive. As Maurice Freedman pointed out, the key to the viability of the Chinese lineage was in its internal stratification and in the existence within such descent groups of an elite class:

Since the effective leaders of the differentiated lineage were neither appointed by nor under the orders of the magistrate, and since if they were themselves scholars they could confront the magistrate on an equal footing, the will of the state could be restricted without a breach of administrative duty. Unless he was prepared to bring in the militia, the magistrate could only deal and treat with a recalcitrant lineage; he could not command it. By preventing a bureaucrat from serving in his own province the system attempted to avoid nepotism and corruption; but by allowing lineage leadership to take on a strong bureaucratic colouring without imposing any bureaucratic checks upon it, the state weakened its control of the lineage, however much it may have suffused its leadership with the correct ideology. With the gentry as a buffer, the differentiated lineage could oppose itself to the state and yet maintain its standing in official eyes (1958: 138).

While the Tungus, Tiv, and Chinese all make use of a patrilineal descent principle in the organization of descent groups, the ways in which they employ this principle differ considerably. It would be very difficult to imagine how a Chinese lineage of the sort described above could possibly emerge and thrive in an egalitarian, hunting-gathering context. On the other hand, the Chinese lineage illustrates that descent groups per se need not be incompatible with either stratification or strong, centralized states.

It is undoubtedly true that a vastly heterogeneous society cannot be handled or organized solely in terms of kinship—that some new cement must be introduced to hold kinship and local groups together. The stratified state with its monopoly over the use of force arose to perform such a vital integrating function. But the evolution of human society has not simply involved a process of replacement; it seems to have been rather one of accumulation and modification. New elements have been added at each stage in our general transformation and old ones have been modified to meet new conditions and requirements. When stratification appeared in human society the death knell for kinship in general, or for the descent group in particular, was not necessarily sounded as some have suggested. In some places kinship structures have been modified and elaborated in such a way as to accommodate and reflect new conditions.

9

Systems
of
Kinship Nomenclature

The functioning of societies depends upon the presence of patterns for reciprocal behavior between individuals or groups of individuals. The polar positions in such patterns of reciprocal behavior are technically known as *statuses*. . . . It . . . is quite correct to speak of each individual as having many statuses, since each individual participates in the expression of a number of patterns. . . . A Status, as distinct from the individual who may occupy it, is simply a collection of rights and duties. . . . A *rôle* represents the dynamic aspect of a status (Linton 1964: 113–14).

Implicit in the phrases "social organization" and "social structure" is the assumption that human behavior is not random or unpredictable but is rather in some way patterned, and that this behavioral regularity has duration over time. As Ralph Linton put it,

society must . . . develop more or less conscious patterns of what the behavior of individuals in certain positions should be so that it will have guides to the training of these individuals (1964: 99).

These positions and the expected patterns of behavior associated with them are what Linton called, respectively, statuses and roles. Statuses are positions and roles are their behavioral counterparts. Both are abstractions from real behavior. No status exists in isolation; the teacher has his pupil and the doctor his patient. Status and role render behavior predictable; one knows what to expect and how to behave with respect to a mother, a judge, a priest. Every individual in society occupies a number of statuses and plays an equal number of roles. One may be an engineer at the office, a father and husband at home, a lieutenant in the naval reserve on Thursday nights, a patient in the dentist's office on Monday morning, and an uncle when a nephew visits. The terms used to describe various statuses signal behavioral expectancies; when a person performs the role of a professor, he adopts a demeanor and behavior that is both appropriate and expectable. In the same sense one knows what to expect from someone who is a father, a granddaughter, or an aunt. The most important statuses (and status terms) in primitive societies are those defined in terms of kinship position although, as we will later see, such statuses (and terms) are not the only ones possible. Because so much of behavior in primitive society is defined in terms of kinship, anthropologists have given special attention to kinship terminology and its significance, and it is for this reason that we now turn our attention to this subject.

Anthropologists have for some time been interested in the way people refer to their relatives because the terms they use can provide information about other aspects of culture and behavior. The particular combination of kinship terms that people employ is not accidental. Nomenclature systems exhibit an internal logic and consistency such that, given certain bits of information, one can predict other attributes of the system as well as features of cultural behavior and social organization. Some time ago, G. P. Murdock suggested that kinship terminology is the aspect of social structure that is most resistant to change. Its nature is primarily determined by the kinds of family and kin groups present in society, which are in turn shaped by the prevailing rule of residence—the aspect of social structure least resistant to the influence of "external influences" (Murdock 1949: 201–2, 221–22). Murdock was convinced that "the prevailing rule of residence is the point of departure for nearly all significant changes in social organization" (1949: 202; see also Tyler 1889; Lowie 1961; and Titiev 1943). Disharmonies may be produced between the rule of residence, the nature of family and kin groups, and the character of kinship terminology if changes affecting the rule of residence have not yet made themselves felt in other areas of social structure. There may be a time-lag as one aspect of social organization adjusts to another (Murdock 1949: 222; cf., Morgan 1909: 408; White 1959: 133; Lowie 1961: 155; and Dole 1972: 156–158). Where we find a system of kinship terms that seems out of place, where some aspects of usage appear to violate a prevailing model, or where the model itself seems to have changed, such discoveries

may indicate that earlier conditions and social characteristics have changed
or that society is in the process of transformation. Robert Murphy (1967)
has also pointed out that such incongruities may also indicate hidden
aspects of behavior. Kinship terms, according to Murphy,

> may also serve to mask and counterfeit social relationships and thus
> function to conceal from their users the social system as it actually
> operates (1967: 164).

In the course of analyzing the kinship terminology of the Tuareg of Niger
in relationship to their social system, Murphy discovered several apparent
disharmonies. The type of kinship terminology did not seem to fit the
kinds of marriage preferences expressed. Murphy discovered what seemed
to be a remarkable flexibility in the application of kin terms, a flexibility
that led him to believe that "terms may be adapted to conduct rather
than conduct to terms" (1967: 167). Although the patrilineal Taureg were
"supposed to" marry matrilateral cross cousins, for example, they sometimes married parallel cousins. When they did so, however, these cousins
were referred to as matrilateral cross cousins!

In short, kinship terminology can reflect and reveal many aspects of
social behavior and social organization and, for these same reasons, the
study of nomenclature systems can also be of practical value to those
interested in problems of culture change or ethnohistorical reconstruction
(see, for example, Eggan 1937; Spoehr 1947; and Brunner 1955). In this
chapter we will examine the various nomenclature systems that people
throughout the world employ and we will discuss only a few of the things
that one may learn from them.

A few words concerning the use of familiar English kinship terms
might be helpful at this point. The student will notice that when describing nomenclature systems throughout this chapter terms familiar to members of our culture are used. Many anthropologists have abandoned this
form of presentation in favor of using native terms or even systems of
abstract symbols. They have done so because they feel that translating
foreign terms into English equivalents (like father, mother, son, niece,
etc.) might lead one to conclude, without sufficient justification, that
certain fundamental psychological processes are at work. If father and
father's brother are both referred to by the term "father," for example,
one might be tempted to conclude that Ego has generalized attitudes
acquired with respect to father to father's brother (or perhaps *vice-versa*).
I fully agree with those who insist that such a psychological extension of
sentiments has not yet been satisfactorily demonstrated and that all we
would be entitled to conclude from a terminological equation of the two
kin types is that, from Ego's point of view, the two relatives have sig-

nificant things in common. Having taken a position with those who warn against a premature assumption of sentiment extension one way or the other, I nonetheless prefer to use familiar English terms to illustrate nomenclature systems because I have found that most students grasp the differences between systems more readily when this method of presentation is employed.

Origins of Anthropological Interest in Kinship Terminology

Our awareness that many people classify their relatives differently from ourselves is quite old. At least as early as the sixteenth-century, travelers and explorers were amused by strange terminological usages. It was discovered, for example, that some people use a single kinship term to refer to their fathers and uncles, and another common term for their mother and aunts. Instances were also found in which adults referred to infants with terms appropriate for parents, and to cousins with terms suitable for siblings, offspring, or even for the children of siblings. But the first organized attempt to deal with the varied phenomenon of kinship terminology was probably that of the nineteenth-century evolutionist, Louis Henry Morgan (1870). In the course of studying the customs and ways of the Iroquois, Morgan found that these American Indians employed a kinship classification quite different from our own. He was so intrigued with this discovery that he mailed questionnaires soliciting data on kinship terminology to missionaries and colonial administrators throughout the world. Morgan gathered information on 139 societies and, on the basis of his analysis of this data, he concluded that there is an important and fundamental difference between the nomenclature systems of "primitive" and "civilized" peoples—the former tend to employ what Morgan called "classificatory" kinship systems whereas civilized peoples prefer "descriptive" systems. Morgan meant by this that most primitive peoples do not terminologically distinguish Ego's line of descent from collateral lines of descent; they do not distinguish between Ego's siblings and his cousins, or between his parents and their siblings (Figure 9-1 contrasts one possible descriptive system with one possible classificatory one).

Morgan believed that there is a relationship between type of kinship nomenclature system used and stage of evolutionary development (as did many other thinkers of his time). According to the evolutionary scheme that Morgan accepted, humankind originally lived in completely promiscuous groups. Because siblings engaged in sexual relations, and because people could not distinguish their own biological parents from other adults, it was customary to refer to all males and females of the ascend-

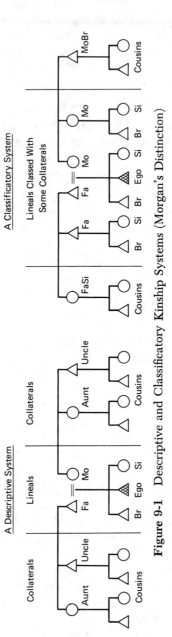

Figure 9-1 Descriptive and Classificatory Kinship Systems (Morgan's Distinction)

128

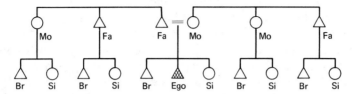

Figure 9-2   The Most "Primitive" Classificatory System of Kinship
Terminology (Morgan's View)

ing generation with terms appropriate for parents. Morgan believed that
this type of classification (see Figure 9-2) was the most primitive of all.

At the other evolutionary pole is our own kinship system. Being
thoroughly "civilized" we have no difficulty distinguishing our parents
from their siblings and our siblings from our cousins, and our enlighten-
ment in this regard is reflected in our kinship terminology (see the descriptive system illustrated in Figure 9-1). Since the time of Morgan scholars
have debated the evolutionary significance of kinship terminology and
descriptions of existing systems been considerably refined. We have
also discovered that while there are indeed a limited number of nomenclature systems actually in use, each can be found among both "primitive"
and "civilized" peoples. This realization has led many scholars to entirely
reject the notion that there is a relationship between the way people
classify their relatives and the level of their technological, social, political,
or economic development. Although most anthropologists now agree that
there is no *direct* linkage between level of societal complexity and system
of kinship nomenclature, a case can be made for an indirect connection
between the two, as we will see shortly. Before considering further the
evolutionary significance of kinship terminology, however, we should first
familiarize ourselves with the major nomenclature systems found in the
world, and we should also consider the sorts of social and cultural
phenomena they may reflect.

Kin Types, Types of Terms, and
Types of Kinship Nomenclature Systems

It is important to distinguish kinship positions, or "kin types," from the
"terms" that people employ when referring to, or when addressing, the
occupants of such positions. Father and father's brother constitute distinct kin types with respect to a particular Ego although, among some
people, a single term will customarily be used to refer to both relatives.

Mother and mother's brother's son's daughter are also different kin types but, as we will see, some people find enough in common between them to justify the use of a single kinship term.

In constructing kinship nomenclature systems, anthropologists normally gather information about the terms that people use when *referring* to particular kinds of relatives, or kin types, in the presence of a third party. We elicit a term of reference by asking an informant, "what is the relationship between so-and-so and yourself?" The informant may then tell us that so-and-so is his "uncle," or his "mother's brother." There is an important difference between such terms and terms of address, the terms that Ego employs when *addressing* a particular relative. Terms of reference are more consistent from context to context than those used in address and the latter are often metaphorically extended to nonkinsmen. A young person in our own society addressing his father may employ the term "dad," or "pop." But he may also employ the same terms when addressing elderly men other than his biological father, just as he may sometimes address nonsiblings as "brothers" and "sisters." If a foreign anthropoligist studying our own society were to draw inferences about the nature of our society exclusively from terms of address he might erroneously conclude that the members of a particular church group or lodge were children of a single parent since they address each other with terms appropriate for siblings. An anthropologist visiting a Chinese community might be similarly surprised to discover that young people may address all adults of their parents' generation in their village using terms appropriate for uncles and aunts. Possible confusion is avoided when we elicit terms of reference, and it is for this reason that anthropologists prefer to analyze nomenclature systems that have been established on the basis of such terms.

The number of different kinship nomenclature systems found in the world is quite limited. In terms of the manner in which uncles and aunts are treated there are only four major systems—bifurcate-merging, bifurcate-collateral, generational, and lineal. If one considers the way cousins are classified one finds that people everywhere adopt one of six possible systems—Iroquois, Crow, Omaha, Eskimo, Hawaiian, or Sudanese (named after peoples employing each system). The relationship between systems defined in terms of uncle-aunt terms and those defined in terms of the way cousins are classified is indicated in Table 9-1.

As Table 9-2 indicates, although the basic systems of kinship terminology listed in Table 9-1 are limited in number, they do not all occur with the same frequency. For reasons that are not yet entirely clear, Iroquois and Hawaiian are far more common than other types of kinship classification.

Table 9-1

Name of System (focus uncles-aunts)	Name of System (focus cousins)
Bifurcate-Merging	Iroquois Omaha Crow
Bifurcate-Collateral	Sudanese
Generational	Hawaiian
Lineal	Eskimo

Table 9-2   RELATIVE FREQUENCY OF MAJOR KINSHIP
NOMENCLATURE SYSTEMS*

System	Number	Percent of Total
Iroquois	113	25
Omaha	45	10
Crow	36	8
Sudanese	36	8
Hawaiian	144	32
Eskimo	73	16
Totals	447	100

* Based on Coult and Habenstein 1965: 506.

Bifurcate-Merging Terminology

The term "bifurcate-merging" refers to the fact that *some* uncles and aunts are terminologically equated to (or "merged" with) parents while others are terminologically distinguished from (or "bifurcated" from) parents (the classificatory system in Figure 9-1 comprises one example). The figures in Table 9-3 indicate that bifurcate-merging terminology (Iroquois, Omaha, and Crow) is significantly associated with the presence of unilineal descent groups. Societies with unilineal descent are more likely to adopt some form of bifurcate-merging terminology than are societies that lack such descent groups. Conversely, societies with bifurcate-merging terminology are significantly more likely to have unilineal descent groups than societies with other kinship nomenclature systems.

Named after Indians of the North American continent, Iroquois terminology is found in virtually every populated area of the world and is by far the most common form of bifurcate-merging terminology (see Table 9-2). Iroquois is usually found in association with unilineal descent groups of

Table 9-3   Kinship Terminology and Unilineal Descent*

| Kinship System | Type of Society | |
	Unilineal	Other
Omaha	43	2
Iroquois	90	23
Crow	33	3
Sudanese	5	31
Eskimo	17	56
Hawaiian	59	85
Totals	247	200

* Based on Coult and Habenstein 1965: 506.

either the patrilineal or matrilineal variety. When we examine the way in which relatives are classified in an Iroquois system (see Figure 9-3), we find that kinship terms reflect a basic distinction between people who are members of Ego's descent group and people belonging to other descent groups. The fact that one term groups Fa with FaBr, and the fact that FaBrChi are classed with siblings may indicate that the members of each class of relatives have something in common. In a patrilineal society they are all members (distinguished by generation) of Ego's patrilineal descent group. Mother and her sister (with whom she is grouped terminologically) are members of another descent group. The children of MoSi are grouped with siblings since Ego classes their Mo with his own. In a matrilineal system the fact that Mo and MoSi are terminologically grouped reflects their membership in a common matrilineal descent group, and since they are so grouped it follows that their children (i.e., Ego's siblings and his matrilateral parallel cousins) are also classed together. The fact that father and his brothers are terminologically grouped may reflect their membership in a common descent group, and since the offspring of one's FaBr

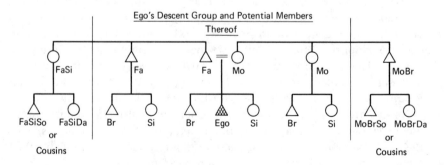

Figure 9-3   An Iroquois Kinship Nomenclature System

are the children of a "father," they are terminologically equated with siblings.

Where unilineal descent groups play a major role in mediating access to the means or the fruits of production, or where descent groups are especially important for other reasons, we often find this reflected in kinship terminology. Omaha terminology signals the presence of strong and highly functional patrilineal descent groups while Crow suggests the presence of strong matrilineal descent groups. Table 9-4 indicates that if

Table 9-4   OMAHA TERMINOLOGY AND PATRILINEAL DESCENT*

	Type of Terminology	
Principle of Descent	Omaha	Other
Patrilineal	42	135
Other	3	267

* Based on Coult and Habenstein 1965: 506.

a society has Omaha terminology, one can safely guess that it is also patrilineal, but if a society is patrilineal it need not classify relatives in terms of an Omaha system. Table 9-5 reveals comparable information about

Table 9-5   CROW TERMINOLOGY AND MATRILINEAL DESCENT*

	Type of Terminology	
Principle of Descent	Crow	Other
Matrilineal	25	47
Other	11	364

* Based on Coult and Habenstein 1965: 506.

Crow terminology. Societies with this system of kinship nomenclature are most likely to be matrilineal even though most matrilineal societies do not have Crow kinship systems.

In both Omaha and Crow societies, Ego is especially concerned about the members of his own descent group—people with whom he shares certain obligations, rights, and privileges and with whom his interactions are especially frequent and important. Because his relations with members of the descent group of his in-marrying parent are less frequent and less vital, the fine terminological distinctions made between members of his own descent group need not be made with respect to the members of this other descent group. For Ego it is important only that these people are members of the descent group of an in-marrying parent, and this is

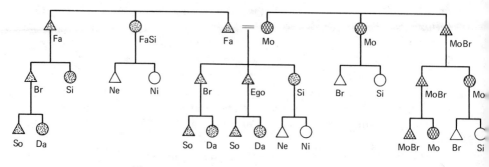

Figure 9-4   An Omaha Kinship Nomenclature System

reflected by the terms of reference that Ego employs with respect to them (see Figures 9-4 and 9-5). In both systems all same-sex members of the in-marrying parents' descent group are equated, *regardless of generation.* The fact that, in an Omaha system, Ego refers to his MoBrSoDa by a term appropriate to mother does not indicate confusion on his part—he is not mistaking what may be a child-in-arms for his own parent. The term "mother" simply indicates a female of his FaWi's descent group. Similarly, in the Crow system, Ego is not confusing MoHu with FaSiDaSo because he refers to both with a term appropriate to father. The term "father" may simply reflect the fact that both individuals are males of Ego's MoHu's descent group.

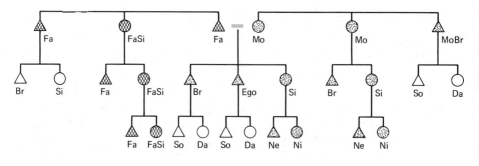

Figure 9-5   A Crow Kinship Nomenclature System

The systemic quality of kinship nomenclature can be made readily apparent through a few examples. Why are BrChi in Omaha referred to by terms appropriate to son and daughter (see Figure 9-4)? Or how do these children refer to Ego? Since they use the term for father (Ego is their FaBr), Ego must reciprocate by referring to them as son and daughter. Why does Ego refer to his SiChi as nephew and niece? Since they refer to him as MoBr (or uncle), he must refer to them by the reciprocal of uncle. Ego refers to his FaSiChi by the same terms for similar reasons Since these children refer to Ego's father by a term appropriate to MoBr, and because the children of a MoBr are invariably also referred to as MoBr and Mo, Ego (being their MoBr) must refer to them as nephew and niece. In the Crow system (see Figure 9-5) we find a similar internal consistency. Why does Ego in Crow refer to his MoBrChi as son and daughter? He does so because his mother is their FaSi; and the children of a FaSi in Crow are referred to as father or father's sister. Since they refer to him with a term appropriate to father, he must refer to them with terms appropriate to offspring.

Bifurcate-Collateral Terminology

In a bifurcate-collateral (Sudanese) kinship system all uncles, aunts, and cousins are referred to by different terms—different kinship statuses are not terminologically classed together (see Figure 9-6). In other words collateral relatives are distinguished ("bifurcated") from lineal relatives as well as from each other. Table 9-6 indicates that although most patrilineal societies do not employ a Sudanese system of kinship terminology, societies that do are usually patrilineal. We have yet to discover why this

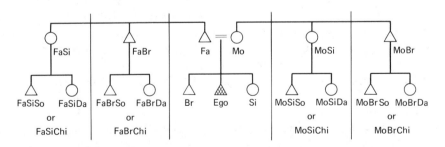

Figure 9-6   A Sudanese Kinship Nomenclature System

Table 9-6   SUDANESE TERMINOLOGY AND PATRILINEAL DESCENT[*]

	Type of Terminology	
Principle of Descent	Sudanese	Other
Patrilineal	30	147
Other	6	264

[*] Based on Coult and Habenstein 1965: 506.

type of terminology is so often associated with patrilineal descent and we have yet to determine the factors that might dispose a patrilineal society to adopt a Sudanese system of kinship classification rather than an Omaha or Iroquois system (see page 142 below for a further discussion of this point).

Lineal Terminology

Lineal (Eskimo) terminology usually signals the presence of some form of cognatic kinship. As Table 9-7 indicates, although most bilateral or

Table 9-7   ESKIMO TERMINOLOGY AND COGNATIC KINSHIP SYSTEMS[*]

	Type of Terminology	
Type of Kinship System	Eskimo	Other
Bilateral or Ambilineal	56	118
Other	17	256

[*] Based on Coult and Habenstein 1965: 506.

ambilineal societies do not make use of Eskimo terminology, societies that do are usually either bilateral or ambilineal in organization. We commonly find Eskimo terminology where people do not adhere to a strict unilocal rule of postmarital residence and where emphasis is placed on the nuclear family rather than on the extended family or descent group. As Figure 9-7 indicates, the members of Ego's nuclear family are distinguished from all other relatives. Nonlineal relatives on both the maternal and paternal sides are classed together with distinctions among them being made only in terms of sex and generation. The manner of classifying relatives suggests that Ego considers himself equally related to all nonlineal relatives—a suggestion of bilaterality. Lineal systems are most commonly found in either very simple societies in which nuclear families

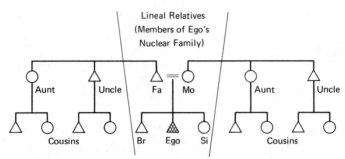

Figure 9-7 An Eskimo Kinship Nomenclature System

comprise the major exploitative units, or in very complex societies, like our own, where economic forces encourage a similar emphasis on the nuclear household (Textor 1967).

Generational Terminology

Where a consistent unilocal mode of postmarital residence is absent or has been abandoned, generational (Hawaiian) rather than lineal (Eskimo) kinship classification may be found. As Table 9-8 indicates, societies with Hawaiian terminology, like those with Eskimo systems, are most often either bilaterally or ambilineally organized. If we examine Figure 9-8, we find that no terminological distinctions are made between relatives on the paternal and maternal sides. Hawaiian terminology is often found in societies with extended families and/or corporate ambilineal descent groups (Textor 1967). It is very likely that Hawaiian nomenclature is especially suited to situations in which there are important cognatically organized corporate groups larger and more inclusive than the nuclear family (e.g., bilaterally organized extended families and/or descent groups). The fact that Ego does not terminologically distinguish between his parents and their siblings, or between his own siblings and his cousins (except in

Table 9-8 HAWAIIAN TERMINOLOGY AND COGNATIC KINSHIP SYSTEMS*

	Type of Terminology	
Type of Kinship System	Hawaiian	Other
Bilateral or Ambilineal	85	89
Other	59	214

* Based on Coult and Habenstein 1965: 506.

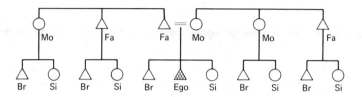

Figure 9-8   A Hawaiian Kinship Nomenclature System

terms of sex), may indicate that any of these relatives may also be members of important corporate groups to which Ego belongs.

The terms of reference that comprise any system of kinship nomenclature are clearly not accidental; terminologies exhibit an internal logic and consistency, and reflect characteristics of the societies in which they are found. We have seen that the kinds of groups present in society may influence the type of nomenclature that will be adopted. Some scholars have suggested that other factors may exert an influence on kinship terminology.

Kinship Terminology and Historical Accident

Kinship terminology, according to some researchers, is a product of historical accident; the kinship terms that a particular people employ and societal changes affecting these terms are mainly the result of cultural borrowing and of modifications imposed upon indigenous systems by local conditions. Alfred Kroeber, a proponent of this view, described a finite series of logical distinctions that could be employed in the construction of a nomenclature system—for example, distinctions in terms of age, sex, generation, or collateral line (1909). Kroeber never suggested a set of rules that might enable us to predict *which* distinctions a particular people would employ. This is understandable in terms of his conviction that kinship terminology is essentially a matter of historical accident. G. P. Murdock pointed to a major flaw in this "historical" approach to kinship terminology. He noted that where cultural phenomena may take an infinite number of forms, where there is no limitation on the number of possibilities, cross-cultural similarities may usually be attributed to diffusion. But where the forms of behavior are limited, similarities should be expected in many societies irrespective of historical accidents and connections (or the lack of them). The specific kinship terms that people employ clearly vary from society to society, but the methods of classification are few. Since there are only a limited number of terminological systems we must assume that we are not dealing with an accident prone phenomenon (Murdock 1949: 113–17).

Kinship Terminology and Language

Some scholars consider kinship nomenclature to be more a linguistic than a social phenomenon—that the terms people employ are a function of their language above all else (see, for example, Gifford 1940: 193–94). The particular terms that people employ must conform in structure to the principles underlying their language but the way in which relatives are *classified* does not have any necessary relationship to these principles. As Murdock pointed out, it is no accident that we find the same type of kinship classification among peoples speaking different languages, just as we may find different nomenclatures being employed by peoples who speak the same language (1949: 117–18). Since this is so we must reject the view that there is something inherent in language that determines the way in which kinsmen will be classified.

Psychology and Kinship Terminology

Alfred Kroeber once suggested that, "terms of relationship reflect psychology, not sociology" (1909: 84). What he meant was that kinship terms reflect a way of thinking and that nomenclature systems are predicated upon certain fundamental psychological processes. We can assume that certain relatives are referred to by the same term because they are thought of as being similar in crucial ways. To the extent that psychological principles apply to *all* humans, however, they cannot account for cultural differences. As we indicated earlier, it is not possible to account for cultural variation in terms of factors that are invariable or universal. If different kinship nomenclature systems reflect *different* psychological processes, on the other hand, then it is important that we ultimately discover why people vary in terms of the processes that guide their thought (Murdock 1949: 119–20).

Sociological Principles and Kinship Terminology

Radcliffe-Brown attempted to account for differences in kinship terminology in terms of certain "fundamental principles or tendencies which appear in all societies, or in all those of a certain type" (1952: 18). Bifurcate-merging terminology, for example, was attributed to the operation of a principle that Radcliffe-Brown called, "the social equivalence of brothers":

> The principle of classification that is most commonly adopted in primitive society may be stated as that of the equivalence of brothers. In other words if I stand in a particular relation to one man I regard myself as standing in the same general kind of relation to his brother; and similarly with a woman and her sister. In this way the father's brother comes to be regarded as a sort of father, and his sons are, therefore, relatives of the same kind as brothers. Similarly, the mother's sister is regarded as another mother, and her children are therefore brothers and sisters (1952: 18; see also 1931: 429).

The problem is that Radcliffe-Brown fails to indicate the conditions under which people will or will not conceptually equate siblings. Clearly not all people do equate them. Hawaiian terminology is supposedly understandable in terms of another principle, the "principle of generation." And when people disregard generation in the classification of relatives this reflects operation of the "principle of unity of the sib" (or descent group). Apart from the obviously tautological character of these principles there is also the crucial and unanswered question of under what conditions one or the other suggested principle is likely to take precedence (Murdock 1949: 121).

Rules of Marriage and Kinship Terminology

Some scholars have proposed a connection between kinship classification and the rules of marriage a people employ (see, for example, Aginsky 1935: 450–51; Gifford 1916: 186–88; Lesser 1929: 722–25; Lowie 1930: 102–8; or Sapir 1916: 327–37). When certain marriage customs produce a situation in which Ego can trace relationship to someone in more than one way (or might eventually be able to do so), then there will be a tendency to refer to these different kinship statuses by means of a single term. Assume, for example, that a people express preference for levirate marriage. If a woman is encouraged to marry the brother of her deceased husband there will be a tendency to terminologically equate FaBr with Fa because the former is potentially a MoHu. In the case of the sororate, there will be a tendency to equate MoSi with Mo since the former is potentially FaWi. But, as Murdock pointed out, customs of preferential marriage should influence kinship terminology only if they apply to all or at least most of the marriages contracted by members of a particular society. Since levirate and sororate marriages are actually relatively rare, it is unlikely that they would determine the kinship usages of an entire society. To top matters off, ethnographic evidence fails to confirm the alleged correlation between levirate and sororate marriage, on the one hand, and bifurcate-merging terminology, on the other. Not all bifurcate-merging systems encourage these forms of marriage, and bifurcate-merging terminology is not characteristic of all societies that do encourage levirate and sororate marriage (Murdock 1949: 123–24).

Kinship Terminology and Evolution

Most anthropologists seem to agree that there is no *direct* relationship between type of nomenclature system and level of societal complexity measured in technological, economic, social, or political terms. This is undoubtedly what Murdock had in mind when he observed that,

> the forms of social organization, indeed, appear to show a striking lack of correlation with levels or types of technology, economy, property rights, class structure, or political integration. . . . An objective classification of societies in terms of their similarities in social structure results in grouping together under the same specific type and sub-type such dissimilar peoples as the New England Yankees and the forest-dwelling Negritoes of the Andaman Islands. . . . Nowhere does even a revised evolutionism find a shred of support (1949: 187).

Cross-cultural studies indicate that all systems of kinship nomenclature are to be found in societies of all degrees of cultural complexity. Even the evolutionist, Leslie White, felt compelled to admit that no one since the time of Morgan had been able to formulate a convincing theory of the evolution of kinship systems (White 1959: 135), and one of White's more famous students, Elman Service, wrote:

> That the relationship of kinship terminologies to social structure is not simple and direct is obvious in the fact that some very different kinds of societies have the same kind of kinship terminology and some rather similar societies have very dissimilar terminologies. It is even more obvious when we scan the total range of culture evolution, from simple bands to complex civilization, that kinship terminologies do not themselves evolve in any sense from simple to complex. In fact, there is no apparent directional change at all, hence kin terminology cannot be considered a reflection of the society in any direct sense (1962: 186–187).

If we consider complexity of political integration to be an index of general societal complexity then, as Table 9-9 shows, all systems of kin-

Table 9-9   KINSHIP NOMENCLATURE AND POLITICAL COMPLEXITY*

Type of Kinship Nomenclature	Level of Political Integration		
	Absence of Political Integration or Autonomous Local Communities not Exceeding 1,500 in Population	Peace Groups Transcending Local Community where Basis of Unity is Other than Political† or Minimal States from 1,500 to 10,000 in Population	States with Populations of 10,000 and Over
Iroquois	62	23	22
Omaha	21	15	9
Crow	20	12	4
Sudanese	3	12	19
Eskimo	28	6	31
Hawaiian	69	39	25

* Based on data in Murdock 1967.

† E.g., derived from trade relations, military agreements, or common cult or age-grade organization.

ship classification are indeed to be found in societies of all degrees of complexity. In other words, one cannot accurately predict which nomenclature system will occur simply on the basis of political complexity. But if we contrast certain specific kinship nomenclature systems with others, and relate this contrast to a trichotomized classification of societies in terms of political complexity (using a χ^2 test for significance), then certain statistically significant associations do appear between kinship classification and political (societal) complexity. Bifurcate-merging systems (Iroquois, Omaha, and Crow), for example, seem to be associated with politically less complex societies. Bifurcate-collateral (Sudanese) systems manifest an opposite association—they are more likely to be associated with politically more complex societies, although it is not clear why this should be the case. Adoption of Sudanese nomenclature makes possible fine distinctions among the members of a common descent group and, for this reason, Sudanese may be more common than bifurcate-merging terminology in societies that have functional descent groups and in which class stratification and occupational specialization are well developed (i.e., in politically more complex unilineal societies). There is some statistical evidence that Sudanese terminology is in fact associated with unilineal societies that have class stratification and occupational specialization, while bifurcate-merging terminology is not (Textor 1967; cf., Dole 1965).

Lineal (Eskimo) systems seem to exhibit a curvilinear association with respect to level of political integration (see Table 9-9.) This kind of terminology appears to be less common in societies of mid-range political complexity than in those that are either politically very simple or very complex. This should not be particularly surprising since the nuclear family and/or household (with which Eskimo terminology is associated) are likely to be stressed in such societies.

Generational (Hawaiian) systems appear to be equally likely to occur at any level of political complexity. Lineal and generational systems are associated with bilocality or neolocality rather than with a fixed rule of postmarital residence, and are associated with the presence of exclusively cognatic kin groups (Textor 1967). Hawaiian terminology may be especially characteristic of cognatically organized societies that possess important kin groups larger than the nuclear family-household. The figures in Table 9-10 indicate that ambilineal descent groups are significantly more

Table 9-10   HAWAIIAN KINSHIP NOMENCLATURE AND
AMBILINEAL DESCENT*

Type of Kinship System	Ambilineal Descent	
	Predominent	Not Predominent
Hawaiian	34	219
Other	17	591

* Data Based on Murdock 1967.

likely to be found in association with Hawaiian kinship systems than with any other nomenclature systems, and there is also evidence that Hawaiian terminology is associated with societies that have extended families (Textor 1967).

Elman Service recently provided a different perspective on the relationship between kinship nomenclature and level of evolutionary development (1960a and 1962: 185–95). He attempted to account for the fact that all terminological systems are found in societies of all degrees of complexity, and to suggest some reasons for the fact that we frequently do not find certain nomenclature systems where we might expect to. Why, for example, do we not always find Omaha kinship classification in association with strong patrilineal descent groups? The essence of Service's speculation is that kinship terminology is *only one kind of status terminology*. Kinship nomenclature is what Service prefers to call "egocentric-familistic" status terminology. All terms are distributed with respect to a specific ego and are linked to kinship. But other systems of status terminology are possible and do occur. Sociocentric-familistic terms, for example, are also linked to kinship but the reference is society rather than a specific ego. The terms "father" and "brother," when used to refer to Catholic religious specialists, constitute examples of sociocentric-familistic status terms. A Catholic priest is a "father" and a Catholic monk is a "brother" with respect to all members of society. To say that a certain Chinese is a "Hwang," a member of the Hwang descent group, is similarly to employ a sociocentric-familistic categorization since everyone would refer to him as a Hwang. Egocentric-nonfamilistic terms comprise another category of status terms. In this case the specific terms employed bear no relationship to kinship position but are ego-specific. "My maid" is not your maid, just as "my Lord" (in a feudal context) is not your Lord. Sociocentric-nonfamilistic terms are those which are neither associated with kinship position nor ego-specific. Doctor, General, and Chief are terms of this sort—they bear no relationship to kinship and have relevance to all members of society.

The trouble is, according to Service, that scholars have been talking not about how *status terms* relate to evolutionary level, but only about how certain status terms (i.e., those that are egocentric-familistic) do. Service draws our attention to an article by Anthony F. C. Wallace (1961) which points out that the semantic complexity of kinship nomenclature systems shows no variation which can be correlated to societal complexity; nomenclature systems are *equally* complex in societies of all levels of complexity. But Wallace also indicates that other taxonomic systems (like verb paradigms, phonemic alphabets, etc.) in any culture also fall within certain ranges of complexity. The fact that no taxonomic system contains more than 2^6 (or 64) entities suggests that the human mind may not be equipped to absorb and retain more complex taxonomic systems. If there is such a limitation on semantic complexity, speculates Service, then as cultures become increasingly complex, and as the kinds of status positions proliferate, people must add *new* taxonomic subsystems rather than increasingly complicate older ones. Thus, growing societal complexity could not be accommodated indefinitely in terms of egocentric-familistic terminology:

> If it be accepted that kinship terminologies are kinds of status terms, and if it be accepted that evolution typically (or, at least, often) consists of a multiplication of parts rather than total replacement of one part by another, so that the old can be retained in the new, then some important possibilities logically follow. Different kinds of status terminologies themselves may come into being successively and directionally, in the manner characteristic of the succession of stages in the general evolutionary perspective (1962: 185; cf., 1960a).

The evolution of human society and culture has been in the direction of increasing complexity and growing heterogeneity. This trend, according to Service's speculation, has involved a proliferation of status positions as well as of status terms. Since nomenclature systems are limited in terms of the number of entities they may contain, new kinds of status terminologies must be generated to accommodate this increasing complexity. The process is essentially additive rather than replacive. Kinship terms continue to be used although kinship distinctions may become less important than other kinds of status distinctions, such as those that refer to membership in particular groups, to rank, or to occupation. Although Morgan believed that Hawaiian terminology reflected the promiscuity of most primitive society, in the light of Service's speculation it is not surprising to find that tribal societies, like the Cheyenne and the Nuer, have Hawaiian systems. In both of these societies important status terms are based upon criteria other than kinship (e.g., age-set membership in the case of the Nuer and warrior society membership in the case of the Cheyenne). Hawaiian society was ranked and stratified and this complexity was reflected in a multitude of nonfamilistic status terms. In a similar vein, Robert Murphy has pointed out that,

> the beauty of Hawaiian terminology—and probably one of the reasons for its recurrence in Oceania and among societies experiencing radical change—is that it is a *nonsystem*, for by lumping all kin of a generation together it departs from the primary taxonomic functions of differentiation and merging. It is ideally adapted to societies in which kinsmen must be acknowledged as such, but in which the mode and content of the relationships are not readily predictable (1967: 169–70).

From this point of view, then, it would be a mistake to link such diverse peoples as the Eskimo and the New England Yankees (as Murdock has done) simply because they share a common kinship terminology. As Service pointed out,

> there *are* some similarities between Eskimo families and New England families, and in their respective egocentric terminology, but obviously the societies as wholes, and their status terminologies in general, are almost polar extremes of dissimilarity (1960a: 760).

Another anthropologist, Gertrude Dole, has insisted that if we consider only systems of egocentric-familistic terminology in relation to level of societal complexity, it is possible to discern associations of evolutionary significance. With respect to Eskimo terminology in particular, Dole notes that many scholars have focused upon the terms used in referring to cousins and have not given sufficient attention to differences in the classification of other relatives. But when one considers these relatives it becomes apparent that not all the systems that Murdock considered Eskimo are really found in societies at all levels of cultural complexity (1960, 1972). It is true that wherever Eskimo terminology is employed there does seem to be a particular emphasis on the distinctiveness of the nuclear family and its constituent primary relatives (i.e., father, mother, brother, sister, son, and daughter). But just as Yankee, Eskimo, and Andaman societies differ in complexity, their respective versions of Eskimo terminology also differ. The Andamanese and Eskimo rely more than the Yankee on both collateral and lineal kinsmen for social security. This is reflected in the fact that one finds considerable terminological merging of kin statuses beyond the group of primary relatives. Dole summarizes her comparison of Eskimo variants as follows:

> Yankee nomenclature is also of an isolating nature. I have referred to it as Modern Isolating to indicate this fact and also that it differs from both the Eskimo and the Andaman patterns in every generation. . . . The differences may be summarized as follows: (1) Instead of classing together lineal and collateral relatives in the grandparent and grandchild generations as do the Primitive [e.g., Andaman] and Secondary [e.g., Eskimo] Isolating, Modern Isolating nomenclature differentiates *all* lineal from collateral relatives. This is because property is inherited primarily in a lineal pattern, and because an individual is not responsible for the support and protection of his collateral relatives. (2) In its more precise form, the Modern Isolating pattern expresses differences in degrees of consanguinity among collateral relatives in each generation, which is not true of the Primitive or Secondary Isolating. The function of this feature is to differentiate between relatives according to inheritance rights, especially to subsistence property. (3) Finally, the Modern Isolating pattern groups together collateral relatives of different generations, whereas each generation is terminologically distinct in both the Primitive and Secondary Isolating patterns. In industrial society many people have almost no contact with offspring of their parents' siblings. When this is true, it is not likely that they will be concerned enough with more distant relatives to differentiate them with special nomenclature (1960: 175).

In a later study (1972) of over 700 kinship systems, Dole found evidence of a correlation between various (refined) nomenclature types and size of autonomous local groups, types of kin groups, residence practices, types of exogamous units, preferential marriage practices, rules of descent, and inheritance of subsistence property—all features that can also be used to distinguish and discriminate levels of cultural complexity. Nomenclature systems were also found to correlate with a sequence of political, economic, and subsistence features ranging from simple to complex. Because of the complexity of Dole's argument it would not be appropriate for us to pursue or evaluate it here. Her analysis did lead her to agree with Murdock's assertion that "there is no inevitable sequence of social forms" for any *particular* society (Murdock 1949: 200). However, although societies can evolve or devolve in complexity,

> in the development of culture as a whole there is a tendency among kinship nomenclatures and structures to change in regular and predictable ways in response to a general increase in cultural complexity (Dole 1972: 161).

It should be clear from all that has been said thus far that while the study of kinship terminology promises to contribute much to our understanding of human behavior and culture change, we still have much to learn about what determines variation in the way people classify their kinsmen, and that the issue of the relationship between kinship nomenclature and societal complexity is also far from resolved.

Conclusion

We have come a long way from the days when our paleolithic forebearers hunted animals and collected plants to keep alive. We have conducted social experiments in virtually all corners of the earth and have, thus far at least, demonstrated an impressive flexibility and inventiveness. Not all of our social experiments have been entirely successful, but we have managed to come to terms with each other and with nature generally. But then again we are still at the beginning. If this discourse on human kinship and social organization serves no other purpose, I hope that it at least indicates that our behavior is neither accidental nor random, and that the determinants of human behavior are both discoverable and knowable. Although we are at the beginning in this regard as well, the progress that has already been made should be sufficient to convince us that we can contribute to our own continued survival by better understanding the sources and potentials of our behavior. Perhaps this modest effort will constitute a contribution to that understanding, even if only by what it has left hanging and unexplained.

References

ABERLE, D. 1961 "Matrilineal Descent in Cross-Cultural Perspective," in D. Schneider and K. Gough (eds.), *Matrilineal Kinship*. Berkeley: University of California Press, pp. 655–727.

ABERLE, DAVID F., URIE BRONFENBRENNER, ECKHARD H. HESS, DANIEL R. MILLER, DAVID M. SCHNEIDER, and JAMES N. SPUHLER 1963 "The Incest Taboo and the Mating Patterns of Animals," *American Anthropologist* 65: 253–65.

ADAMS, M. and J. V. NEIL 1967 "Children of Incest," *Pediatrics* 40: 55–62.

ADAMS, RICHARD N. 1960 "An Inquiry into the Nature of the Family," in G. E. Dole and R. L. Carneiro (eds.), *Essays in the Science of Culture*. New York: Thomas Y. Crowell, pp. 30–49.

AGINSKY, B. W. 1935 "The Mechanics of Kinship," *American Anthropologist* 37: 450–51.

ALLAND, ALEXANDER 1972 *The Human Imperative*. New York: Columbia University Press.

ANDERSON, ROBERT 1971 "Voluntary Associations in History," *American Anthropologist* 73: 209–22.

ARDREY, ROBERT 1961 *African Genesis*. New York: Dell Publishing.
_____1966 *The Territorial Imperative*. New York: Dell Publishing.
_____1970 *The Social Contract*. New York: Atheneum.

BARTH, FREDRIK 1954 "Father's Brother's Daughter Marriage in Kurdistan," *Southwestern Journal of Anthropology* 10: 164–71.

BEFU, HARUMI 1968 "Origins of Large Households and Duolocal Residence in Central Japan," *American Anthropologist* 70: 309–19.

BENDER, DONALD R. 1967 "A Refinement of the Concept of Household: Families, Co-Residence, and Domestic Functions," *American Anthropologist* 69: 493–504.

———1971 "De Facto Families and De Jure Households in Ondo," *American Anthropologist* 73: 223–41.

BLUMBERG, RAE LESSER and ROBERT F. WINCH 1972 "Societal Complexity and Familial Complexity: Evidence for the Curvilinear Hypothesis," *American Journal of Sociology* 77: 898–920.

BOHANNAN, PAUL 1954 "The Migration and Expansion of the Tiv," *Africa* 24: 2–16.

———1958 "Extra-Processual Events in Tiv Political Institutions," *American Anthropologist* 60: 1–12.

———1963 *Social Anthropology*. New York: Holt, Rinehart & Winston.

BOYER, RUTH 1964 "The Matrifocal Family among the Mescalero: Additional Data," *American Anthropologist* 66: 593–602.

BROWN, PAULA 1964 "Enemies and Affines," *Ethnology* 3: 335–56.

BRUNER, EDWARD 1955 "Two Processes of Change in Mandan-Hidatsa Kinship Terminology," *American Anthropologist* 57: 840–49.

CARNEIRO, ROBERT L. 1968a "Slash-and-Burn Cultivation among the Kuikuru and its Implications for Cultural Development in the Amazon Basin," in Y. A. Cohen (ed.), *Man in Adaptation: The Cultural Present*. Chicago: Aldine, pp. 131–45 (originally published in 1961).

———1968b "The Transition from Hunting to Horticulture in the Amazon Basin," in Y. A. Cohen (ed.), *Man in Adaptation: The Cultural Present*. 2d ed. Chicago: Aldine, pp. 157–66.

———1970 "A Theory of the Origin of the State," *Science* 169: 733–38.

———1974 "The Four Faces of Evolution," in J. J. Honigmann (ed.), *Handbook of Social and Cultural Anthropology*. Skokie, Ill.: Rand McNally, pp. 89–110.

CLINGET, REMI and JOYCE SWEEN 1974 "Urbanization, Plural Marriage, and Family Size in Two African Cities," *American Ethnologist* 1: 221–42.

COHEN, MYRON L. 1967 "Variations in Complexity among Chinese Family Groups: The Impact of Modernization," *Transactions of the New York Academy of Sciences* 29: 638–44.

COHEN, MYRON L. 1968 "A Case Study of Chinese Family Economy and Development," *Journal of Asian and African Studies* 3: 161–80.

———1970 "Developmental Process in the Chinese Domestic Group," in M. Freedman (ed.), *Family and Kinship in Chinese Society*. Stanford: Stanford University Press, pp. 21–36.

COHEN, YEHUDI A. 1969 "Ends and Means in Political Control: State Organization and the Punishment of Adultery, Incest, and Violation of Celibacy," *American Anthropologist* 71: 658–87.

CONDOMINAS, GEORGES 1973 "The Primitive Life of Vietnam's Mountain People," in R. A. Gould (ed.), *Man's Many Ways*. New York: Harper and Row, pp. 199–226.

COULT, ALLAN D. and ROBERT W. HABENSTEIN 1965 *Cross Tabulations of Murdock's World Ethnographic Sample*. Columbia, Mo.: University of Missouri Press.

DA MATTA, ROBERTO 1972 "A Reconsideration of Apinayé Social Morphology," in Daniel R. Gross (ed.), *Peoples and Cultures of Native South America*. New York: Doubleday/The Natural History Press, pp. 277–89.

DAVENPORT, WILLIAM 1959 "Nonunilineal Descent and Descent Groups," *American Anthropologist* 61: 557–73.

DIVALE, WILLIAM T. 1972 "Systemic Population Control in the Middle and Upper Palaeolithic: Inferences Based on Contemporary Hunter-Gatherers," *World Archaeology* 4: 222–43.

———1974 "Migration, External Warfare, and Matrilocal Residence," *Behavior Science Research* 9: 75–133.

DOLE, GERTRUDE E. 1960 "The Classification of Yankee Nomenclature in the Light of Evolution in Kinship," in G. E. Dole and R. L. Carneiro (eds.), *Essays in the Science of Culture*. New York: Thomas Y. Crowell, pp. 162–78.

———1965 "The Lineage Pattern of Kinship Nomenclature: Its Significance and Development," *Southwestern Journal of Anthropology* 21: 36–62.

———1972 "Developmental Sequences of Kinship Patterns," in P. Reining (ed.), *Kinship Studies in the Morgan Centennial Year*. Washington, D. C.: The Anthropological Society of Washington, pp. 134–66.

DURKHEIM, ÉMILE 1898 "La Prohibition de L'Inceste et ses Origines," *L'Année Sociologique* 1: 1–70.

DYSON-HUDSON, N. 1966 *Karimojong Politics*. Oxford: Clarendon Press.

EGGAN, FRED 1937 "Historical Changes in the Choctaw Kinship System," *American Anthropologist* 39: 34–52.

———1966 *The American Indian*. Chicago: Aldine.

EMBER, CAROL R. 1974 "An Evaluation of Alternative Theories of Matrilocal Versus Patrilocal Residence," *Behavior Science Research* 9: 135–49.

———(in press) "Residential Variations Among Hunter-Gatherers," *Behavior Science Research* cited with permission of author.

EMBER, CAROL R. and MELVIN EMBER 1972 "The Conditions Favoring Multilocal Residence," *Southwestern Journal of Anthropology* 28: 382–400.

EMBER, CAROL R., MELVIN EMBER, and BURTON PASTERNAK 1974 "On the Development of Unilineal Descent," *Journal of Anthropological Research* 30: 69–94.

EMBER, MELVIN 1967 "The Emergence of Neolocal Residence," *Transactions of the New York Academy of Sciences* 30: 291–302.

———1974a "The Conditions That May Favor Avunculocal Residence," *Behavior Science Research* 9: 203–9.

———1974b "Warfare, Sex Ratio, and Polygyny," *Ethnology* 13: 197–206.

———1974c "On the Origin and Extension of the Incest Taboo," *Behavior Science Research* (forthcoming).

EMBER, MELVIN and CAROL R. EMBER 1971 "The Conditions Favoring Matrilocal Versus Patrilocal Residence," *American Anthropologist* 73: 571–94.

ENGELS, FREDERICK 1942 *The Origins of the Family, Private Property, and the State*. New York: International Publishers.

EVANS-PRITCHARD, E. E. 1970 "Sexual Inversion among the Azande," *American Anthropologist* 72: 1428–34.

EYDE, DAVID and PAUL M. POSTAL 1961 "Avunculocality and Incest: The Development of Unilateral Cross-Cousin Marriage and Crow-Omaha Kinship Systems," *American Anthropologist* 63: 747–71.

FORTES, MEYER 1953 "The Structure of Unilineal Descent Groups," *American Anthropologist* 55: 17–41.

FOX, R. 1967 *Kinship and Marriage: An Anthropological Perspective*. Baltimore: Penguin Books.

FREEDMAN, MAURICE 1958 *Lineage Organization in Southeastern China*. London: The Athlone Press.

———1966 *Chinese Lineage and Society: Fukien and Kwangtung*. New York: Humanities Press.

———1970 "Ritual Aspects of Chinese Kinship and Marriage," in M. Freedman (ed.), *Family and Kinship in Chinese Society*. Stanford: Stanford University Press, 163–87.

FREUD, S. 1931 *Totem and Taboo*. New York: New Republic.

FRIED, MORTON H. 1957 "The Classification of Corporate Unilineal Descent Groups," *The Journal of the Royal Anthropological Institute* 87: 1–29.

_____1967 *The Evolution of Political Society*. New York: Random House.

_____1968 "On the Evolution of Social Stratification and the State," in M. H. Fried (ed.), *Readings in Anthropology*. 2d ed., vol. 2. New York: Thomas Y. Crowell, 462–78. Originally published in 1960.

GEERTZ, CLIFFORD 1963 *Agricultural Involution*. Berkeley: University of California Press.

GIFFORD, E. W. 1916 "Miwok Moieties," *University of California Publications in American Archaeology and Ethnology* 12: 186–88.

_____1940 "A Problem in Kinship Terminology," *American Anthropologist* 42: 190–94.

GLASS, ROBERT and MERVYN MEGGITT (eds.) 1969 *Pigs, Pearlshells, and Women: Marriage in the New Guinea Highlands*. Englewood Cliffs, N. J.: Prentice-Hall.

GOGGIN, JOHN M., and WILLIAM C. STURTEVANT 1964 "The Calusa: A Stratified Nonagricultural Society (With Notes on Sibling Marriage)," in W. H. Goodenough (ed.), *Explorations in Cultural Anthropology: Essays in Honor of George Peter Murdock*. New York: McGraw-Hill, pp. 179–219.

GOLDSCHMIDT, WALTER 1966 *Comparative Functionalism*. Berkeley: University of California Press.

GOLDSTEIN, M. C. 1971 "Stratification, Polyandry, and Family Structure in Central Tibet," *Southwestern Journal of Anthropology* 27: 64–74.

GOODE, WILLIAM J. 1963 *World Revolution and Family Patterns*. London: The Free Press of Glencoe.

_____1967 "Goode's Reply to Otterbein," *American Anthropologist* 69: 226–27.

GOODENOUGH, WARD H. 1955 "A Problem in Malayo-Polynesian Social Organization," *American Anthropologist* 57: 71–83.

GOUGH, E. KATHLEEN 1968 "The Nayars and the Definition of Marriage," in P. Bohannan and J. Middleton (eds.), *Marriage, Family and Residence*. New York: Doubleday Natural History Press, pp. 49–71. Originally published in 1959.

GRANQVIST, HILMA 1931 "Marriage Conditions in a Palestinian Village," *Helsingfors, Commentationes Humanarum, Societas Scientarium Fennica* 3.

GREENFIELD, SIDNEY M. 1961-62 "Industrialization and the Family in Sociological Theory," *American Journal of Sociology* 67: 312–22.

GROSS, DANIEL R. 1971 "The Great Sisal Scheme," *Natural History* 53: 48–55.

GULLIVER, P. H. 1968a "The Jie of Uganda," in Y. A. Cohen (ed.), *Man in Adaptation: The Cultural Present.* 2d ed. Chicago: Aldine, pp. 323–45.

————1968b "The Turkana," in Y. A. Cohen (ed)., *Man in Adaptation: The Cultural Present.* 2d ed. Chicago: Aldine, pp. 346–61.

HAMMEL, E. A. 1961 "The Family Cycle in a Coastal Peruvian Slum and Village," *American Anthropologist* 63: 989–1005.

HANSON, ALLAN F. 1970 "The Rapan Theory of Conception," *American Anthropologist* 72: 1444–47.

HARRIS, MARVIN 1959 "The Economy Has No Surplus?" *American Anthropologist* 61: 185–99.

————1971 *Culture, Man, and Nature.* New York: Thomas Y. Crowell.

HAYANO, DAVID M. 1974 "Marriage, Alliance, and Warfare: A View from the New Guinea Highlands," *American Ethnologist* 1: 281–93.

HOEBEL, E. ADAMSON 1960 *The Cheyennes: Indians of the Great Plains.* New York: Holt, Rinehart and Winston.

HOMANS, G. and D. M. SCHNEIDER 1955 *Marriage, Authority and Final Causes.* New York: Free Press.

ITANI, JUN'ICHIRO 1961 "The Society of Japanese Monkeys," *Japan Quarterly* 8: 421–30.

JOHNSON, ERWIN 1964 "The Stem Family and its Extension in Present Day Japan," *American Anthropologist* 66: 839–51.

JOSSELIN DE JONG, J. P. B. 1971 "Presumed Behavior: Comments on Cara E. Richards' Brief Communication," *American Anthropologist* 73: 270–73.

KIRCHHOFF, PAUL 1968 "The Principles of Clanship in Human Society," in M. H. Fried (ed.), *Readings in Anthropology.* 2d ed., vol. 2. New York: Thomas Y. Crowell, 370–81. Originally published in 1955.

KLOOS, PETER 1963 "Marital Residence and Local Endogamy: Environmental Knowledge or Leadership," *American Anthropologist* 65: 854–62.

KROEBER, A. 1909 "Classificatory Systems of Relationship," *Journal of the Royal Anthropological Institute* 39: 77–84.

KUMMER, HANS 1971 *Primate Societies.* Chicago: Aldine-Atherton.

KUNSTADTER, PETER 1963 "A Survey of the Consanguine or Matrifocal Family," *American Anthropologist* 65: 56–66.

LANG, OLGA 1946 *Chinese Family and Society.* New Haven: Yale University Press.

LEACH, E. R. 1961 "The Structural Implications of Matrilateral Cross-Cousin Marriage," in *Rethinking Anthropology.* London: The Athlone Press, pp. 54–104.

LEE, RICHARD B. 1969 "Kung Bushmen Subsistence: An Input-Output Analysis," in Andrew P. Vayda (ed.), *Environmental and Cultural Behavior.* New York: Doubleday Natural History Press, pp. 47–79.

LEE, RICHARD B. and I. DE VORE (eds.) 1968 *Man the Hunter.* Chicago: Aldine.

LERNER, I. MICHAEL 1958 *The Genetic Basis of Selection.* New York: John Wiley and Sons.

LESSER, A. 1929 "Kinship Origins in the Light of Some Distributions," *American Anthropologist* 31: 710–30.

LEVI-STRAUSS, C. 1949 *The Elementary Structures of Kinship.* Boston: Beacon Press.

LEVY, M. J. and L. A. FALLERS 1959 "The Family: Some Comparative Considerations," *American Anthropologist* 61: 647–51.

LINTON, RALPH 1952 "Cultural and Personality Factors Affecting Economic Growth," in B. F. Hoselitz (ed.), *The Progress of Underdeveloped Areas.* Chicago: University of Chicago Press, pp. 73–88.

———1964 *The Study of Man.* New York: Appleton-Century-Crofts. Originally published in 1936.

———1968 "The Natural History of the Famliy," in M. H. Fried (ed.), *Readings in Anthropology.* 2d ed., vol. 2. New York: Thomas Y. Crowell, 277–95. Originally published in 1947.

LIVINGSTONE, FRANK B. 1969 "Genetics, Ecology and the Origins of Incest and Exogamy," *Current Anthropology* 10: 45–61.

LORENZ, KONRAD 1966 *On Aggression.* New York: Harcourt Brace Jovanovich.

LOWIE, ROBERT H. 1930 "The Omaha and Crow Kinship Terminologies," *Proceedings of the International Congress of Americanists* 24: 102–8.

———1961 *Primitive Society.* New York: Harper. Originally published in 1920.

MALINOWSKI, B. 1922 *Argonauts of the Western Pacific.* New York: E. P. Dutton.

———1929 *The Sexual Life of Savages.* London: George Routledge.

———1931 "Culture," in *Encyclopedia of the Social Sciences* 4: 630.

MARTIN, M. KAY 1969 "South American Foragers: A Case Study in Cultural Devolution," *American Anthropologist* 71: 243–60.

MAUSS, MARCEL 1954 *The Gift.* London: Cohen and West.

MAYBURY-LEWIS, DAVID 1960 "Parallel Descent and the Apinayé Anomoly," *Southwestern Journal of Anthropology* 16 (2).

MAYER, P. 1950 "Privileged Obstruction of Marriage Rites among the Gusii," *Africa* 20: 113–25.

McLENNAN, J. F. 1865 *Primitive Marriage.* Edinburgh: Adam and Charles Black.

MEAD, MARGARET 1968 "The Structure of Mundugumor Society," in Paul Bohannan and John Middleton (eds.), *Kinship and Social Organization.* New York: Doubleday The Natural History Press, pp. 225–31.

MEGGERS, BETTY J. 1954 "Environmental Limitations on the Development of Culture," *American Anthropologist* 56: 801–24.

_____1960 "The Law of Cultural Evolution as a Practical Research Tool," in G. Dole and R. Carneiro (eds.), *Essays in the Science of Culture.* New York: Thomas Y. Crowell, pp. 302–16.

MEGGITT, M. J. 1968 " 'Marriage Classes' and Demography in Central Australia," in R. B. Lee and I. De Vore (eds.), *Man the Hunter.* Chicago: Aldine-Atherton, pp. 176–84.

MONTAGU, M. F. ASHLEY 1968 *Man and Aggression.* New York: Oxford University Press.

MOORE, F. W. 1961 *Readings in Cross-Cultural Anthropology.* New Haven, Conn.: Human Relations Area Files Press.

MORGAN, L. H. 1870 *Systems of Consanguinity and Affinity of the Human Family.* Washington, D. C.: Smithsonian Institution.

_____1909 *Ancient Society.* Chicago: Chas. H. Kerr.

MORRIS, DESMOND 1967 *The Naked Ape.* New York: McGraw-Hill.

MORRIS, H. S. 1959 "The Indian Family in Uganda," *American Anthropologist* 61: 779–89.

MORTON, NEWTON E. 1961 "Morbidity of Children from Consanguineous Marriages," in A. G. Steinberg (ed.), *Progress in Medical Genetics* vol. 1, 261–91. New York: Grune and Stratton.

MULLER, JEAN-CLAUDE 1973 "On Preferential/Prescriptive Marriage and the Function of Kinship Systems: The Rukuba Case (Benue-Plateau Site, Nigeria)," *American Anthropologist* 75: 1563–76.

MURDOCK, GEORGE P. 1949 *Social Structure.* New York: Macmillan.

_____1957 "World Ethnographic Sample," *American Anthropologist* 59: 664–87.

_____1967 *Ethnographic Atlas.* Pittsburgh: University of Pittsburgh Press.

MURPHY, ROBERT F. 1967 "Tuareg Kinship," *American Anthropologist* 69: 163–70.

———and LEONARD KASDAN 1959 "The Structure of Parallel Cousin Marriage," *American Anthropologist* 61: 17–29.

NAROLL, RAOUL 1956 "A Preliminary Index of Social Development," *American Anthropologist* 58: 687–715.

———1970 "What Have We Learned from Cross-Cultural Surveys?" *American Anthropologist* 72: 1227–88.

NEEDHAM, R. 1962 *Structure and Sentiment.* Chicago: University of Chicago Press.

NIMKOFF, M. F. and RUSSELL MIDDLETON 1960 "Types of Family and Types of Economy," *American Journal of Sociology* 66: 215–25.

ODUM, EUGENE P. 1963 *Ecology.* New York: Holt, Rinehart and Winston.

ORENSTEIN, HENRY 1956 "Irrigation, Settlement Pattern, and Social Organization," in *Selected Papers of the Fifth International Congress of Anthropological and Ethnological Sciences.* Philadelphia: University of Pennsylvania Press, pp. 318–23.

OSMOND, MARIE W. 1965 "Toward Monogamy: A Cross-Cultural Study of Correlates of a Type of Marriage," *Social Forces* 44: 8–16.

OTTERBEIN, KEITH F. 1965 "Caribbean Family Organization: A Comparative Analysis," *American Anthropologist* 67: 66–79.

———1969 "Basic Steps in Conducting a Cross-Cultural Study," *Behavior Science Notes* 4: 221–36.

———1970a "The Developmental Cycle of the Andros Household: A Diachronic Analysis," *American Anthropologist* 72: 1412–19.

———1970b *The Evolution of War: A Cross-Cultural Study.* New Haven, Conn.: Human Relations Area Files Press.

OTTERBEIN, KEITH F. and CHARLOTTE SWANSON OTTERBEIN 1965 "An Eye for an Eye, A Tooth for a Tooth: A Cross-Cultural Study of Feuding," *American Anthropologist* 67: 1470–82.

PARSONS, TALCOTT 1955 "The American Family: Its Relations to Personality and to the Social Structure," in T. Parsons and R. F. Bales (eds.), *Family, Socialization and Interaction Process.* New York: Free Press, pp. 3–33.

PASTERNAK, BURTON 1972a *Kinship and Community in Two Chinese Villages.* Stanford: Stanford University Press.

———1972b "The Sociology of Irrigation: Two Taiwanese Villages," in W. E. Willmott (ed.), *Economic Organization in Chinese Society.* Stanford: Stanford University Press, pp. 193–213.

RADCLIFFE-BROWN, A. R. 1931 "Social Organization of Australian Tribes," *Oceania* 1: 429.

_____1952 *Structure and Function in Primitive Society.* New York: Free Press.

RICHARDS, CARA E. 1969 "Presumed Behavior: Modifications of the Ideal-Real Dichotomy," *American Anthropologist* 71: 1115–17.

RITTER, MADELINE L. 1974 *The Conditions Favoring Age-Set Organization.* M.A. Thesis, Department of Anthropology, Hunter College of the City University of New York.

ROSEN, BERNARD C. and MANOEL T. BERLINCK 1968 "Modernization and Family Structure in the Region of São Paulo, Brazil," *América Latina* 11: 75–96.

ROSENFELD, HENRY 1957 "An Analysis of Marriage Statistics for a Moslem and Christian Arab Village," *International Archives of Ethnography* 48: 32–62.

SAHLINS, M. D. 1958 *Social Stratification in Polynesia.* Seattle: University of Washington Press.

_____1960 "Evolution: Specific and General," in M. D. Sahlins and E. R. Service (eds.), *Evolution and Culture.* Ann Arbor: University of Michigan Press, pp. 12–44.

_____1961 "The Segmentary Lineage: An Organization of Predatory Expansion," *American Anthropologist* 63: 322–45.

_____1963 "Poor Man, Rich Man, Big-Man, Chief: Political Types in Melanesia and Polynesia," *Comparative Studies in Society and History* 5: 285–303.

_____1965 "On the Sociology of Primitive Exchange," in *The Relevance of Models for Social Anthropology.* Association for Social Anthropologists Monograph 1. New York: Frederick A. Praeger.

SAPIR, E. 1916 "Terms of Relationship and the Levirate," *American Anthropologist* 18: 327–37.

SCHNEIDER, D. M. and E. KATHLEEN GOUGH (eds.) 1961 *Matrilineal Kinship.* Berkeley: University of California Press.

SELIGMAN, B. Z. 1929 "Incest and Descent," *Journal of the Royal Anthropological Institute* 59: 231–72.

_____1951 *Notes and Queries in Anthropology* (6th ed.) London: Routledge and Kegan Paul.

SERVICE, ELMAN R. 1960a "Kinship Terminology and Evolution," *American Anthropologist* 62: 747–63.

_____1960b "The Law of Evolutionary Potential," in M. D. Sahlins and E. R. Service (eds.), *Evolution and Culture.* Ann Arbor: University of Michigan Press, pp. 93–122.

_____1960c "Sociocentric Relationship Terms and the Australian Class System," in G. E. Dole and R. L. Carneiro (eds.), *Essays in the*

Science of Culture in Honor of Leslie A. White. New York: Thomas Y. Crowell, pp. 416–36.

SERVICE, ELMAN R. 1962 *Primitive Social Organization.* New York: Random House.

———1971 *Profiles in Ethnology* (Revised). New York: Harper and Row.

SLATER, MIRIAM 1959 "Ecological Factors in the Origin of Incest," *American Anthropologist* 61: 1042–59.

SMITH, ARTHUR H. 1970 *Village Life in China.* Boston: Little, Brown and Company. Originally published in 1899.

SMITH, RAYMOND T. 1956 *The Negro Family in British Guiana.* London: Routledge and Kegan Paul.

SOLIEN, NANCIE L. 1960 "Household and Family in the Caribbean," *Social and Economic Studies* 9: 101.

SOLIEN DE GONZALES, NANCIE L. 1965 "The Consanguineal Household and Matrifocality," *American Anthropologist* 67: 1541–49.

SOUTHWICK, CHARLES H. 1972 "Aggression among Nonhuman Primates," *Addison-Wesley Module in Anthropology* 23.

SPENCER, HERBERT 1862 *First Principles.* London: Williams and Norgate.

SPIRO, MELFORD E. 1954 "Is the Family Universal? The Israeli Case," *American Anthropologist* 56: 839–46.

———1958 *Children of the Kibbutz.* Cambridge: Harvard University Press.

SPOEHR, ALEXANDER 1947 "Changing Kinship Systems," *Field Museum of Natural History, Publications, Anthropological Series* 33: 151–235.

SPOONER, BRIAN 1972 *Population Growth: Anthropological Implications.* Cambridge: The MIT Press.

STEWARD, JULIAN H. 1955 *Theory of Culture Change.* Urbana: University of Illinois Press.

———1959 "Prediction and Planning in Culture Change," *Human Organization* 18: 5–7.

———1970 "Cultural Evolution in South America," in W. Goldschmidt and H. Hoijer (eds.), *The Social Anthropology of Latin America.* Los Angeles: Latin American Center, University of California, pp. 199–223.

STRICKON, ARNOLD 1962 "Class and Kinship in Argentina," *Ethnology* 1: 500–15.

SUSSMAN, ROBERT W. 1972 "Child Transport, Family Size, and Increase in Human Population During the Neolithic," *Current Anthropology* 13: 258–59.

SUTTLES, W. 1960 "Affinal Ties, Subsistence and Prestige among the Coast Salish," *American Anthropologist* 62: 296–30.

TALMON, YONINA 1964 "Mate Selection in Collective Settlements," *American Sociological Review* 29: 491–508.

TEXTOR, R. B. (Comp.) 1967 *A Cross-Cultural Summary*. New Haven, Conn.: Human Relations Area Files Press.

TITIEV, MISCHA 1943 "The Influence of Common Residence on the Unilateral Classification of Kindred," *American Anthropologist* 45: 511–30.

TOPLEY, MAJORIE 1955 "Ghost Marriages Among the Singapore Chinese," *Man*, Article 35.

———1956 "Ghost Marriages among the Singapore Chinese: A Further Note," *Man*, Article 63.

TYLOR, E. B. 1889 "On a Method of Investigating the Development of Institutions: Applied to Laws of Marriage and Descent," *Journal of the Royal Anthropological Institute* 18: 245–69.

VAN VELZEN, H. U. E. THODEN, and W. VAN WETERING 1960 "Residence, Power Groups and Intra-Societal Aggression," *International Archives of Ethnography* 49: 169–200.

VAYDA, ANDREW P. 1968 "Economic Systems in Ecological Perspectives: The Case of the Northwest Coast," in M. H. Fried (ed.), *Readings in Anthropology*. 2d ed., vol. 2 New York: Thomas Y. Crowell, pp. 172–78.

VICARY, GRACE Q. 1967 "Otterbein, Goode, and the Caribbean Family," *American Anthropologist* 69: 224–26.

WALLACE, ANTHONY F. C. 1961 "On Being Just Complicated Enough," *Proceedings of the National Academy of Sciences* 47: 458–64.

WATSON, JAMES L. 1974 "Restaurants and Remittances: Chinese Emigrant Workers in London," in G. M. Foster and R. V. Kemper (eds.), *Anthropologists in Cities*. Boston: Little, Brown and Company, pp. 201–22.

WESTERMARCK, EDWARD 1894 *The History of Human Marriage*. London: Macmillan.

WHITE, LESLIE A. 1949 *The Science of Culture*. New York: Grove Press.

——— 1959 *The Evolution of Culture*. New York: McGraw-Hill.

WHITING, J. W. M. 1969 "Effects of Climate on Certain Cultural Practices," in W. H. Goodenough (ed.), *Explorations in Cultural Anthropology*. New York: McGraw-Hill.

WILSON, M. 1963 *Good Company: A Study of Nyakyusa Age-Villages*. Boston: Beacon Press.

WITTFOGEL, KARL A. 1957 *Oriental Despotism: A Comparative Study of Total Power*. New Haven, Conn: Yale University Press.

WITTFOGEL, KARL A. 1968 "The Theory of Oriental Society," in M. H. Fried (ed.), *Readings in Anthropology* 2d ed., vol. 2 New York: Thomas Y. Crowell, 179–98.

WOLF, ARTHUR P. 1966 "Childhood Association, Sexual Attraction, and the Incest Taboo: A Chinese Case," *American Anthropologist* 68: 883–98.

———1968 "Adopt a Daughter-in-Law, Marry a Sister: A Chinese Solution to the Problem of the Incest Taboo," *American Anthropologist* 70: 864–74.

———1970a "Childhood Association and Sexual Attraction: A Further Test of the Westermarck Hypothesis," *American Anthropologist* 72: 503–15.

———1970b "Chinese Kinship and Mourning Dress," in M. Freedman (ed.), *Family and Kinship in Chinese Society.* Stanford: Stanford University Press, pp. 189–207.

WOODBURN, JAMES 1968a "An Introduction to Hadza Ecology," in R. B. LEE and I. DE VORE (eds.), *Man the Hunter.* Chicago: Aldine-Atherton, pp. 49–55.

———1968b "Stability and Flexibility in Hadza Residential Groupings," in R. B. Lee and I. De Vore (eds.), *Man the Hunter.* Chicago: Aldine-Atherton, pp. 103–110.

YENGOYAN, ARAM A. 1968 "Demographic and Ecological Influences on Aboriginal Australian Marriage Sections," in R. B. Lee and I. De Vore (eds.), *Man the Hunter.* Chicago: Aldine-Atherton, pp. 185–99.

Index